Getting Started in
Sociology

6th Edition

Edited by Lisa Grey Whitaker

Mc
Graw
Hill
Education

ISBN-13: 978-1-260-40857-7
ISBN-10: 1-260-40857-4

Solutions Program Manager: Kelly Casey
Project Manager: Lisa Haverland
Cover Photo Credits: Digital Vision/Getty Images

Table of Contents for 6th edition of Lisa Whitaker's SOC 101 book

Design Pics/Don Hammond

PART I
The Basics

1

FUNDAMENTAL CONCEPTS AND PERSPECTIVES
LISA GREY WHITAKER

Before you being the other readings in this book, I want to introduce you to some basic sociological concepts. Please note, the definitions of the concepts provided here are *working definitions*. Other sociologists may define the concepts somewhat differently. Referring to these working definitions as you read will help you absorb and understand the material.

What Is Sociology?

Sociology is the study of what individuals and groups do, in relation to each other. Because of that in-relation-to-each-other part, sociologists call the conduct they study interpersonal or *social* behavior. The *other*, referred to in the phrase "in relation to each other," could be one other person in direct physical contact with you. Or, *other* could refer to everyone else in the world, who you are considering in the abstract.

Sociologists say that all the social 'relating' or interaction you have engaged in thus far in your life will affect how you decide to act in the here-and-now. For example, imagine you are in a room by yourself; deciding what to do with some alone-time you have right now. A sociologist would say, you at least *think about* how other people would react if they were to see you engage in the behavior you are contemplating. Because you have at least *considered* how others would react to what you are about to do, even how you act in solitude is, in a sense, social.

Sociologists also study *how* and *why* people behave socially as they do; how and why their behavior changes (or doesn't) over time, and how changes—innovations—in social behavior spread from the few who "invented" the changes, to much larger social groups.

Sociologists may study social behavior and group processes within a single society. Or, they may study these phenomena in two or more societies, then compare the groups.

The size and scope of a sociologist's research project, as well as the methods (s)he uses to do the research, will vary according to the theoretical perspective (s)he adheres to, the types of behavior or processes (s)he is interested in studying and, of course, realities like funding and staff resources.

Depending on the range of persons or groups studied, the length of time they are studied, and which tools a sociologist uses to measure, record and analyze the data (s)he collects, a sociologist is said to 'do' either *macro sociology* or *micro sociology*. Macro sociologists are like photographers who shoot their photos using a wide-angle lens. They would rather fit a lot of people into each frame than get detailed images of just a few of them. By contrast, micro sociologists are like photographers who use a zoom lens. They focus on only a few people at a time so they can capture a lot of detail about each person.

Theoretical Perspectives

Most sociological theories fall into one of three theoretical camps. We call these camps *theoretical perspectives.* Each perspective offers its own view of what society is and how its parts operate vis à vis each other. The substance of each perspective has changed over time due to historical events; political developments and so on. Too, each has sprouted 'spin-off' perspectives, like a hit TV show generates spin-off series.'

Each theoretical perspective houses many, more specific theories; concerning a variety of subject areas within Sociology, e.g. Sociology of Adolescence. Because this is an introductory-course text and you may never take another sociology course again in your life, I do not want to overwhelm you with a zillion different theories. I am just sticking to the basics here; giving you a bare-bones description of each of the three perspectives. Sociologists refer to these as the functionalist, conflict and interactionist perspectives.

Functionalism compares society to the human body. Sociologists call this the *organic analogy.* Functionalists study the parts of society together, as an entire system. If they were to examine any of the parts separately, it would only be to understand how that part contributes to the overall system. Because its unit of analysis is the system as a whole, functionalism is a macro sociological perspective.

Functionalism offers a relatively static view of society. It suggests things must remain as they are—the status quo must be maintained—in order for all parts of society to work together, in balance with each other. Persons or groups who engage in social protest, or who otherwise work to effect social change, are seen as threats to the state of balance in the system. As an example, take the fictional character *Robin Hood.* The Sheriff of Nottingham, obviously a functionalist, viewed Robin as a threat to the status quo he (the Sheriff) was part of. As the Sheriff saw it, Robin had to go. Examples of Functionalist theories are *Structural Functionalism* and the *Boundary Maintenance* theory of deviance.

Conflict Theory is also a macro sociological perspective. The primary focus of conflict theorists is the competition between groups to control resources such as wealth, power and influence. According to conflict theorists, social change is not only good, if not inevitable; it is the way a society progresses.

Earlier conflict theorists saw control of resources as an either-or proposition. Society's members fell into one of two camps—the *haves,* a minority who controlled societal resources, or the *have-nots,* who aspired to wrest control from the *haves,* while scrambling to get what crumbs the 'haves' left behind. Occasionally the *have-nots* managed to displace the *haves,* as occurred during the 1917 Russian Revolution.

Contemporary conflict theory starts with the notion of **interest groups.** Interest groups are persons who act in a cooperative, coordinated fashion. The basis of their cooperation is a common goal. They seek to have an impact on some socio-political issue, concerning which decision(s) are to be made. Examples of interest groups are LGBT individuals, the American Tobacco Association, the American Association of Retired Persons (AARP), political parties, and Feminists.

In relation to the issues they care about, interest groups strive to play a larger role in decision making and acquire greater control over resources that help them advance their causes. At any given point in time there are a number of socio-political issues in play, concerning which something is to be decided. For each of these issues, there is a 'haves' group in charge of the issue and any related resource allocation. At the same time, for each issue one or more 'have-not' groups seek to unseat the dominant group or to at least get a larger share of the pie, where the nature of the 'pie' may simply be an equal voice in decision-making. In this more complicated conception, there exist a myriad of interest-group clusters. The member-groups that make up each cluster duke it out amongst themselves for whatever spoils are to be had, related to 'their' issue.

Neo-Marxist theory, Queer Theory and *Feminist Theory* are examples of contemporary conflict theories. Each of these explicates the ways in which members of the relevant interest group(s) have historically suffered abuse, discrimination and been barred in general from full participation in Society. Each of these perspectives also suggests the types of social change that would need to occur to effect equal treatment and equal participation in society for its members, and suggests strategies for accomplishing these.

From the *interactionist* point of view, the best way to understand what is going on in society is, to start at the ground level and work up. The unit of analysis is the situation – in particular, any of the routine social situations that make up daily life in society. Interactionists analyze the verbal and nonverbal communication between persons who come across one another in everyday situations. They seek to understand the social structure that underlies the communication and makes it seem 'routine.' Because its unit of analysis is the situation and the relatively small number of persons in it, rather than an entire social system, the interactionist perspective is a micro-sociological perspective. Examples of interactionist theories are: *Symbolic Interactionism, Dramaturgy* and *Labeling theory.*

What Is Society?

Sociologists use the term society in a narrower, more technical way than does the average citizen. To sociologists, a *society* is the aggregate of persons who live within a specific, demarcated territory and share at least the basic elements of a single, general culture. Here the word *aggregate* refers to individuals and groups of all sizes and types; living within the designated region. On this same turf may reside individuals and/or groups who are *not* members of the society in question, because they choose to *not* buy into the mainstream culture.

What Is Culture?

A society's *culture* is the stock of knowledge that a resident of or traveler within the society must know and use, in order to 'do' daily life without attracting unwanted forms of attention, such as public ridicule or police contact. The basic building blocks of culture are norms (rules of conduct), *values* (actions or ways of treating other people that are considered desirable, appropriate and/or moral), *language* (verbal and non-verbal communication), *beliefs* (agreements between members about the existence and makeup of each feature of their shared existence), the social *statuses* (positions) a person may occupy and the role played by any person who occupies any one of those statuses.

What Are Social Institutions?

Social institutions are networks of persons whose coordinated, interdependent actions accomplish essential tasks for society's members. These tasks are essential because they enable members to do their lives in accordance with their culture's core values. For example, a principal social institution in most societies is the system of education. In U.S. society, the education system as a social institution makes it possible for members to 'live' the cultural value, "getting a good education."

Government, religion, the family, the education system and the mass media are some of the social institutions in our culture. Essential tasks performed by social institutions include care of the young, socialization of new members, education and training of the youth, dissemination of information, and creation and enforcement of a set of rules for members to live by, so that their daily lives seem to proceed in a more or less orderly fashion.

What Is Social Structure?

For many of you the word *structure* may evoke images of a building under construction; of a solid, tangible framework. For our purposes, though, focus on the word *social*. *Social* structure is not tangible; it's an idea. It's an idea that is formulated through social interaction and then experienced through individual perception and interpretation.

You are aware that social rules and meanings evolve through social interaction. Through discussion, debate, disagreement, compromise and/or consensus, people formulate (and subsequently change or maintain) a collective sense of what *type* of situation this or that piece of their daily lives *is* (e.g., "This is an elevator ride") and of *how to act* ("Face forward and don't look too long at, or talk to, anyone you don't know") within it.

All sorts of *social variables,* such as gender, age, race or profession can affect the amount of influence an individual has on the process of creating, maintaining or changing situational meanings and rules. Some individuals get to talk more than others because of their relatively high status ranking. At the same time, the highest-ranking person may speak only once during a discussion, yet exert great influence on its outcome. Because social variables can have such an impact on the outcome of situation-defining and rule-making encounters, when studying them sociologists look not just at *what* is said but also, at *who* (the status ranking of the person who) is saying it.

Each of us notices the behavior of those around us. To the extent you perceive that those around you are *acting as if* they buy into existing ideas of what certain situations *are* and how to act within them, there is a seeming orderliness to the world, an *apparent* structure to everyday existence. However behind that appearance, at any given moment in time, someone, somewhere is chipping away at this or that little piece of the structure – modifying some rule, working to repeal and/or replace it, etc. Over time people may change all the rules that inform their everyday lives, but – incrementally. Social structure is a work-in-progress. It's a *process*.

Now you're ready to start looking at the world around you as a sociologist. You will be looking beneath the surface of social situations; watching and analyzing the interaction through which people give meaning and a sense of orderliness to their existence.

REFERENCES

Berger, Peter L., *Invitation to Sociology,* Garden City, NY: Doubleday Anchor Books, 1963.

Berger, Peter and Thomas Luckmann, *The Social Construction of Reality;* Garden City, NY: Doubleday, 1967.

Blumer, Herbert, *Symbolic Interactionism: Perspective and Method;* Englewood Cliffs, NJ: Prentice-Hall, 1969

Cooley, Charles Horton, *Human Nature and the Social Order;* New York: Schocken, 1964.

Dahrendorf, Ralf, *Class and Class Conflict in Industrial Society;* Stanford, CA: Stanford University Press, 1959.

Denzin, Norman K., *Symbolic Interactionism and Cultural Studies: The Politics of Interpretation;* Oxford: Blackwell, 1992.

Goffman, Erving, *The Presentation of Self in Everyday Life;* Garden City, NY: Doubleday, 1959.

Mead, George Herbert, *Mind, Self and Society;* University of Chicago Press, Chicago, IL, 1934.

Merton, Robert K., *Social Theory and Social Structure;* New York: Free Press, 1968.

Mills, C. Wright, *The Sociological Imagination;* New York, Oxford University Press, 1959.

Parsons, Talcott, *Sociological Theory and Modern Society;* New York: Free Press, 1967.

Strauss, Anselm et. al., "The Hospital and its Negotiated Order," in E. Freidson (ed.),
   The Hospital and Modern Society, 1963, pp. 147–169.

Weber, Max, *From Max Weber: Essays in Sociology;* Hans Gerth and C. Wright Mills, Eds, New York, Oxford University Press, 1946

2

SOCIALIZATION AND CULTURE
RELATED CONCEPTS AND IDEAS
LISA GREY WHITAKER

Socialization: Learning the Culture

As mentioned in the previous chapter, a society's culture is the stock of knowledge a person must have and regularly use in a society, in order to get through daily life without attracting unwanted forms of attention such as public ridicule or police contact. Newcomers to a society, whether infants, immigrants or temporary visitors, receive the information they need in order to 'do' daily life in their new environment through socialization. Established members of society socialize new arrivals by explaining to them the "who-what-when-where-why-and-how" of their general culture – i.e., the basic building blocks of the culture, which are its norms, values, language(s), beliefs, statuses and roles.

Depending on the basis upon which a newcomer enters the society, (s)he will endeavor to soak up cultural know-how to a greater or lesser degree, as befits his/her personal agenda. Thus an infant born to established members of society, in all likelihood, will be inclined to absorb the culture in depth. An immigrant may fully embrace the new culture, hoping to achieve citizenship in the fullness of time. Or, such a individual may remain faithful to the culture from whence (s)he came; observing its traditions at home; raising his or her children in accordance with its tenets. In that case, an immigrant might elect to learn and adhere to only enough of the host culture to accomplish daily life outside the home.

Persons and social entities who participate in your socialization at various points in time during your life are called *agents of socialization.* Agents include parents and guardians, teachers, your peer group, religious officials, significant others, coaches, bosses, role models, and the mass media including television, movies, the internet, newspapers and magazines.

Many times in the course of your life, you will begin learning how to perform the role that goes with a status you do not yet have, but expect to have in the future. This kind of advance preparation is called anticipatory socialization. When young children watch their mothers and fathers play 'parent,' they are soaking up information about how to be parents themselves, someday. Even though they are not consciously training for the parent role, what they're doing still counts as *anticipatory socialization.*

For those of you who have declared a major, taking courses in your major field is a form of anticipatory socialization. Doing an internship in an organization that is the sort of workplace you expect to work in, following graduation, is anticipatory socialization. If your career goal is to become a dentist, working in a dentist's office or just talking to a number of dentists about how they feel about the work they do, are forms of anticipatory socialization. I'm sure you can think of many times in your life so far, in which you have done this type of role preparation.

Some day you may decide to, or be required to, leave your old life behind and enter an entirely new 'world' with its own unique culture. To survive and do well in that new world, you must undergo *resocialization.* Entry into military service, convents, seminaries, jails, prisons, mental hospitals and some religious sects/cults are examples of self-contained 'worlds' that would require you to be resocialized. Sociologists call self-contained worlds like these *total institutions.*

The Building Blocks of Culture

A *norm* is a rule about how to act, with the word 'act' referring both to what you do and what you say. Norms can be formal or informal. Formal norms are written-down; having been voted on and approved by a governing body, such as a state legislature, and/or the public. Federal, state, or city government's norms are usually called laws or statutes. The formal norms of a specific organization are often called policies and procedures. Informal norms are rules guiding the more mundane aspects of everyday social life. While these rules are not written-down, everyone is familiar with them; having been taught them by our parents and others while we were growing up. An example of an informal norm is the rule about not picking your nose in public.

A *value* is a prospective course of action (e.g. "getting a good education") or an element of the way you treat other people (e.g. "honesty") which members of a culture have generally assessed as good, right, appropriate and/or moral.

Language is the totality of verbal and non-verbal forms of communication a society's members (or a subset of its members) share and use to exchange ideas and information with each other. Language is the medium through which members accomplish crucial processes like socialization, social control and social change, as well as the business of everyday life. Non-verbal forms of language include facial expressions, gestures, tone of voice, posture, bearing, carriage, use of personal space, and general body language. In culturally diverse societies such as ours, members will use a variety of verbal and non-verbal languages; in accordance with their respective cultures of origin and life experiences.

Beliefs are agreements between members of a society about the existence and makeup of each and every feature of their shared experience. Examples of beliefs range from "that thing over there is a tree," to "driving drunk causes accidents," to "the sun will rise tomorrow."

A *status* is a social position — a category, a pigeonhole — created by members of a society, as a way of getting a 'fix' on other people; a way of making sense of who they are. We human beings are always categorizing things and people — defining them, labeling them, evaluating them — as a way of bringing the jumble of everyday life to heel. We are a species determined to create order out of chaos. Boxing people up in neat little categories is one way to do that. Each status carries with it a greater or lesser amount of prestige, according to the values of the society in which it exists. For example, in American society having a career as a physician is more prestigious than having a career as a telemarketer.

From the moment of your birth you have certain *ascribed statuses* — age, race, gender and ethnicity are examples of these. By contrast, your *achieved statuses* are positions you obtain through your own efforts. Examples of achieved statuses you have or may have right now are college student, employee, significant other, athlete, community volunteer or musician.

According to their cultural values, members of a society ascribe a greater or lesser amount of weight — significance — to each status. Citizens of a community may change the weight or importance they assign to a specific status, depending on all sorts of factors — for example, community history, concrete events, local politics or the local economy. Historical, economic and political factors — in other words the larger context in which a set of social statuses exists — will always affect the content and degree of importance that people assign to the statuses they make and use.

In fact, citizens may come to weight one specific status so heavily that once an individual is placed in it, that status overrides any other statuses (s)he may have. Others perceive and interact with the individual only in terms of that one status. Such a status is a master status. A *master status* can be positive (e.g. "Olympic Gold Medalist") or negative (e.g. "child molester"). Our gold medal winner may be conceited or a schmuck; the child molester may be a big-time community philanthropist, but nobody cares. Whatever the individual's additional statuses or attributes may be; however positive or negative, nobody will care anymore — others will see and treat the individual as if (s)he were nothing but that status.

The *role* consists of the duties a status occupant is expected to perform, the mindset (willingness to comply with the norms, values, beliefs, etc. that attach to the status) (s)he is supposed to have, and any privileges (s)he is due to receive, in return for performing the duties. Examples of privileges are the amount of authority or influence (s)he can exercise over others and the amount of prestige (s)he enjoys as an occupant of that status.

Each day you play the variety of roles, which accompany the statuses you occupy that day: daughter or son, sibling, pet owner, commuter, college student, mentor, friend, employee, etc. If you step back and watch yourself one day, you will see there are situations in which you are called upon to play two or more roles simultaneously. For example there you are, sitting in class; trying to pay attention and take notes on the professor's lecture. Right then your friend text-messages you. Playing your role as a friend, to respond to his/her text message, requires a time-out from your student role; the role you are supposed to playing at that moment. When performance of one of role gets in the way of performing another — in other words, when two or more roles collide — the dilemma you feel is called *role conflict.*

There are other occasions when you are playing only one role; however, what you have to do, to perform the role, makes you emotionally uncomfortable. For example, have you ever had to tell your significant other, face-to-face, that you want to break up? Or, have you ever worked as a manager or supervisor and had to tell some of your employees they were being laid off? Any emotional discomfort you feel, out of doing what your role requires you to do, is called *role strain.*

There are times in your life when you finish with a status you have held, more or less for good. For example, you graduate from college and begin a career. You get married. You buy your first house. Here you are leaving behind the statuses of college student, apartment renter and single man or woman. Leaving a status and the role that goes with it is called, imaginatively enough, *role exit.*

Cultures within Cultures: Subcultures and Countercultures

Most of us go through multiple socialization processes during our lives. This occurs because even after you learn the basics of your society's general culture, you will enter additional, more specialized social arenas that are new to you. Such arenas are the settings where members of specific groups within the general society carry out their activities. Such groups could be composed of the members of a club or organization, such as a sports team or a religious organization, persons who practice a particular profession, or just the employees who work at a particular place of business.

To become a full-fledged participant in a group you have just joined, you must absorb a body of knowledge — a culture — which is unique to that group. The group's culture is made of norms, values; any special skills, technical language, clothing or equipment that is required; any belief system that is unique to that group; statuses and their accompanying roles, etc. In other words, they the same building blocks as those which make up the general culture; only the group's culture is specific to that group. It exists as a 'mini'-culture within our much larger, general culture. Sociologists call such mini-cultures either subcultures or countercultures; depending on whether or not the group's members buy into the norms, values and beliefs of the general culture.

A *subculture* is a mini-culture made up of members who adhere to general culture's norms and values, etc., who at the same time also utilize the more specialized set of norms and values, etc. that inform their specific activities. A subculture's members are organized around an activity or set of activities in which they have a heightened level of interest, relative to the population at large. Depending on the size of the social arena in which they operate and the type(s) of activity that have brought them together, the members may or may not have face-to-face contact with each other. For example, the employees of a small, mom-and-pop family restaurant, by interacting with each other face to face, day after day, form a subculture. At the same time, all the professional ballet dancers in the world are also a subculture. Even though most of them will never meet, they share and adhere to a body of knowledge related to their profession. It is their commitment to living in accordance with that body of knowledge that, despite the distances between members, unites them as a subculture.

Sociologists also recognize groups within the general culture whose norms, values and beliefs directly conflict with those of the general culture. Such groups, called *countercultures* by sociologists, reject the norms, values, etc. of the majority and replace them with a set of their own making. The hippies of the 1960's are an oft-cited example of a counterculture.

Many groups, however, do not fit so easily into one category or the other. For example, how do we classify street gangs? Having worked in the justice system for a number of years, I'm aware that members of such gangs display properties of both. Yes; they're okay with killing to settle disputes. On the other hand, most of the gang members I met had very strongly-held 'family values' and religious faiths. How do we categorize groups that have characteristics of both subcultures and countercultures? I suggest we discuss such groups in terms of "the extent to which..." they have subcultural and/or countercultural properties.

REFERENCES

Berger, Peter L. and Thomas Luckmann, The Social Construction of Reality, Garden City, Doubleday, 1967.
Cicourel, Aaron V., "Basic and Normative Rules in the Negotiation of Status and Role," in Hans Peter Dreitzel,
    Recent Sociology, Number 2, 44-49.
Cooley, Charles Horton, Human Nature and the Social Order, New York: Schocken, 1964.
Denzin, Norman K., Symbolic Interactionism and Cultural Studies: The Politics of Interpretation, Oxford: Blackwell, 1992.
Goffman, Erving; Stigma: Notes on the Management of Spoiled Identity, Englewood Cliffs, NJ: Prentice-Hall, 1963.
Mead, George Herbert, Mind, Self and Society, Chicago: University of Chicago Press, 1934.

Ruben Sanchez @lostintv/Getty Images

PART II

Stratification and Social Inequality

3

RELATED CONCEPTS AND IDEAS
LISA GREY WHITAKER

Stratification

Stratification is the categorization and rank-ordering of people according to the amount of some valued personal attribute (e.g. intelligence), social characteristic (e.g. occupation, race, ethnicity, gender), or material resource (referring to both goods and services, e.g. income level, type of car they drive, social club membership) each has, relative to others in the society. Persons who possess roughly the same amount of the valued commodity are placed in a category together. The categories are then rank-ordered. Persons with the most of the valued commodity are in the category at the top; those with the least are in the category at the bottom; those in-between are arranged accordingly.

Social Inequality

What 'caused' members of the earliest human societies to develop systems of stratification in the first place? Harold Kerbo[1] has noted the human inclination to evaluate one's individual attributes, or the social statuses one may have, as being superior or inferior to those of others. Persons with the most highly valued attributes or statuses enjoy access to the most valued forms of, or the largest chunks of, various resources. Once they have a lion's share of resources that others want and/or need, such persons may demand additional resources – goods and services – in return for providing the needy with life's essentials, which those higher up already have in goodly amounts. Out of such dynamics is born *social inequality*, i.e. the inequality of access to valued goods and services, and/or inequality of opportunity to attain certain desirable social statuses; depending on your where you sit in our stratified system.

Obviously, most people would rather own a home than rent (or be homeless); would rather drive their own car to work than take the bus; would rather work in a professional, 'white-collar' position than work on the "kill floor" of a slaughterhouse. Physicians, for example, earn way more than slaughterhouse workers; rendering them in a position to buy nice homes and drive nice cars, especially compared to the means of housing and transportation a laborer can afford.

The norms and values of our culture support this unequal distribution of rewards. The average citizen who was raised in our culture, who assimilated its norms and values, views the income differential between doctors and laborers not just as appropriate, but as 'obvious;' commonsensical. (S)he takes it as a given.

What determines who gets to the top and who is kept down? The functionalists would say the people at the top are there because somehow they deserve to be there. This argument was used in the feudal era to keep the extant monarchies in power, à la the "divine right of kings." With respect to more recent societies, the functionalists would argue that those at the top got there because of their superior intelligence, hard work, significant achievements or contributions; a the-cream-always-rises-to-the-top, Protestant-work-ethic sort of argument.

Historically, major social institutions have contributed to systemic inequality. For example, religious systems have been part of the power structure in certain societies. Religious leaders were thus in a position to suggest that the way things were — the status quo — was God's will. Thus citizens should be content with their portion and aspire neither to higher ground, nor to change society such that the distribution of goods and services was more equitable.

Our system of education perpetuates inequality along gender and racial lines, for example through the use of tracking systems. Earlier on, educators urged boys toward the "hard" sciences and math while detouring girls into home economics and secretarial classes. Federal, state and local governments were for the longest time awash in a sea of white males — who proceeded to allocate, among other things, less funding to school districts in poorer communities than to middle-class districts. Having persisted for years, the inequality in our system became *institutionalized*.

Socialization and Inequality

During socialization, children learn the norms, values and other components of the general culture but also learn those pertaining to particular subcultures, including the subculture of the socioeconomic class into which they are born. While being socialized as a member of a certain socioeconomic class, a child will glean a sense not only of how to act or what to value but also a sense of what goals are/are not appropriate to aspire to; how much/how little (s)he should be content to have.

Thus the very norms and values a child born into a lower socio-economic class may learn, might teach him or her to not hope for, aspire to or expect to have more of the good things in life than the portion (s)he was given at birth. At the same time a child born into an affluent family is socialized to expect a much-expanded gamut of opportunities and privileges. Such socialization at both levels, indeed at any level, only perpetuates the entrenchment of the inequality in our system.

With institutionalized inequality comes institutionalized discrimination and, for the poor, entrapment in a cycle of poverty. Parents who are among the working poor may not be able to afford decent nutrition or decent medical care for themselves or their children when they get sick — especially if their jobs do not yield benefits such as health insurance.

Poor children attend schools in districts with meager resources — outdated textbooks, no computers, etc. Their teachers do not expect them to do well academically and give them that message through their interaction with the children, nonverbally if not verbally. Consequently, many of the children indeed do not do well in school. The standardized achievement tests they take assume a middle-class upbringing and education. Thus students from poorer districts tend to score badly on those tests. Later, their parents cannot afford to put them through college and their academic performance is not sufficient to get them a scholarship. With college not an option, they go to work in the same types of low-level jobs their parents have, without benefits. The cycle continues.

Conflict theorists say the people who are at the top got there by being lucky enough to have been born into the ruling class, or by being the leader of an interest group that wins a struggle for power. Aspirants should be skilled in the arts of persuasion, motivation and manipulation, such that they can wheel and deal their way to the top. Too, their ascendancy can be greased by the influence of powerful friends. Regarding the people who can never seem to get ahead, the conflict theorists would say they are *kept* down deliberately by those higher up, because it serves the interests of the wealthy and/or powerful to *keep* them down. Herbert Gans[2] notes that the poor:

- Provide a low-wage labor pool to do society's "dirty" jobs
- Subsidize a variety of activities for the affluent, for example by serving as guinea pigs in medical research and providing domestic workers (gardeners, housekeepers, servants) who cushion the flow of daily life for the well-to-do
- Create jobs for those in certain occupations which either serve the poor (e.g. pawnshop owners) or protect the rest of society from them (e.g. prison guards)
- Subsidize merchants by buying products that others don't want (e.g. dilapidated housing, produce that is past its prime)
- Serve as a group to be punished in order to reinforce conventional values
- Serve as guarantors of the status(es) of those who are higher up on the social ladder
- Serve as sacrificial lambs (last to be hired, first to be fired or laid off) for the sake of the national economy, in that a certain level of unemployment helps to keep inflation down.

Gans goes on to note[3] that many of these purposes, currently served by the poor, *could* be served by means other than *keeping* them poor. For example, paying decent wages to those who do the dirty jobs would raise them out of poverty. However, to do so would mean those who employ low-wage workers, purchase the products they make or the services they provide would have to shell out more money, which of course they don't want to do. Thus poverty will not be eliminated unless and until it ceases to serve the interests of the wealthy and/or powerful, *or* unless the have-nots, as an interest group, manage to acquire enough (political) power to change the status quo.

Stereotyping, Prejudice and Discrimination

All too often, members of our society have their blinders on when they look at an individual. Despite all the uniqueness and complexity that go into any individual's makeup, others may see this person *only* in terms of the degree to which (s)he possesses a particular attribute, social characteristic or resource. Those others may then assign a whole array of characteristics to this individual, based only on the individual's ranking with respect to this one social commodity. Based on this one factor, the parties sitting in judgment decide the individual is *that kind of* person. Sociologists call such invalid generalizations *stereotyping*.

On the basis of a stereotype others may feel prejudiced toward, and discriminate against, the targeted individual. *Prejudice* is an unfavorable assessment of someone because of his or her assignment to some stereotypical category. *Discrimination* is *acting on* that assessment by unfairly treating, maybe outright abusing the stereotyped person.

You learn stereotypes and acquire your prejudices through socialization and life experience. During your life a multitude of socialization *agents* (including the internet and other media), along with your personal life experiences, will influence how you define and evaluate everything in your world, including other people.

Once learned, why do individuals continue to operate according to their acquired prejudices? Perhaps fear of or discomfort with what is not familiar to them, or with those who are not like them, is the key — or, insecurity within themselves. People who are emotionally secure within themselves do not feel a need to put other people down.

Depending on how early, and from which agents a person acquires his or her prejudices, (s)he may or may not be able to later unlearn them. One way to dismantle a prejudice is to have some new agent come into your life whom you respect and admire; perhaps aspire to be like — a *role model*, for example. If this agent whom you so like and admire does not share your prejudice at all, you may decide to re-think your prejudicial attitudes.

The Contact Hypothesis

Often, stereotypes and prejudices break down when a prejudiced person is required by circumstances to interact one-on-one, over time, in a cooperative fashion, with a member of the group against whom (s)he is prejudiced. For example, an employer may direct two employees who are prejudiced against each other to work on a project as a team. As they interact over time, they get to know each other as individuals. Once they start to see each other's individual qualities, especially the positive ones, the stereotypes start to break down. Our work partners are unable to hang onto their prejudices, at least in regard to each other. The experience starts each of them thinking: "Well...if this one is okay, maybe others in that category are okay, too..." Stereotypes and prejudices do not hold up well under reality-testing. Sociologists' hunch, or expectation, that prejudices break down once the prejudiced parties get to know each other, is called the *contact hypothesis*.

Each of the readings in this section provides a closer look at one specific stratum or group within our society, and at the issues related to being in their place. In *Working and Poor in the USA*, Beth Shulman provides a case study of the cycle of poverty. G. William Domhoff provides a window into upper-class life in *Who Rules America?* Barbara Kantrowitz and Pat Wingert give us an update on affirmative action as applied to college admissions in *What's at Stake*. Finally, in *Civilize Them With a Stick*, Mary Crow Dog (with Richard Erdoes) discusses her experience as a Native American child in a White-run boarding school, in particular how the Whites' best efforts at washing her culture out of her only succeeded at creating "racism in reverse."

ENDNOTES

[1]Harold Kerbo, *Social Stratification and Inequality: Class Conflict in Historical, Comparative and Global Perspective*, 5th edition. New York: McGraw-Hill, 2003, pp.11-13.
[2]Herbert Gans, "The Positive Functions of Poverty;" *American Journal of Sociology*, 78:275-279.
[3]Herbert Gans, "The Uses of Power: The Poor Pay All;" *Social Policy* 2 (July-August 1971):20-24.

REFERENCES

Aguirre, Adalberto Jr. and David V. Baker, *Structured Inequality in the United States: Discussions on the Continuing Significance of Race, Ethnicity and Gender.* Upper Saddle River, NJ: Prentice Hall, 2000.
Davis, Kingsley and Wilbert E. Moore, "Some Principles of Stratification," *American Sociological Review*, 10 (April 1945): 242-249.
Gans, Herbert J., "The Positive Functions of Poverty," *American Journal of Sociology*, 78: 275-279.
_____, "The Uses of Power: The Poor Pay All;" *Social Policy* 2 (July-August 1971):20-24.

Harrington, Michael, *The Other America: Poverty in the United States*. Baltimore: Penguin, 1963.

_____, *The New American Poverty*. NY: Holt, Rinehart and Winston, 1984.

Kerbo, Harold; *Social Stratification and Inequality: Class Conflict in Historical, Comparative and Global Perspective*, 5th edition. NY: McGraw-Hill, 2003.

LeDuff, Charlie, "At a Slaughterhouse, Some Things Never Die," in Susan Ferguson (ed.), *Mapping the Social Landscape: Readings in Sociology*, 4th edition, NY: McGraw-Hill, 2005.

Lenski, Gerhard E.; *Power and Privilege*. NY: McGraw-Hill, 1966.

Tumin, Melvin M; "Some Principles of Stratification," *American Sociological Review* 18 (August 1953):387–393.

_____; *Patterns of Society*. Boston: Little, Brown and Company, 1973.

4

THE SILVER SPOON: INHERITANCE AND THE STAGGERED START
STEPHEN J. MCNAMEE AND ROBERT K. MILLER JR.

To heir is human.

— Jeffrey P. Rosenfeld, *Legacy of Aging*

A common metaphor for the competition to get ahead in life is the foot race. The imagery is that the fastest runner — presumably the most meritorious — will be the one to break the tape at the finish line. But in terms of economic competition, the race is rigged. If we think of money as a measure of who gets how much of what there is to get, the race to get ahead does not start anew with each generation. Instead, it is more like a relay race in which we inherit a starting point from our parents. The baton is passed, and for a while, both parents and children run together. When the exchange is complete, the children are on their own as they position themselves for the next exchange to the next generation. Although each new runner may gain or lose ground in the competition, each new runner inherits an initial starting point in the race.

In this intergenerational relay race, children born to wealthy parents start at or near the finish line, while children born into poverty start behind everyone else. Those who are born close to the finish line need no merit to get ahead. They already are ahead. The poorest of the poor, however, need to traverse the entire distance to get to the finish line on the basis of merit alone. In this sense, meritocracy applies strictly only to the poorest of the poor; everyone else has at least some advantage of inheritance that places him or her ahead at the start of the race.

In comparing the effects of inheritance and individual merit on life outcomes, the effects of inheritance come first, *followed by* the effects of individual merit — not the other way around. Figure 1 depicts the intergenerational relay race to get ahead.

FIGURE 1
The intergenerational race to get ahead. Note: solid lines are effects of inheritance; dashed lines are potential effects of merit.

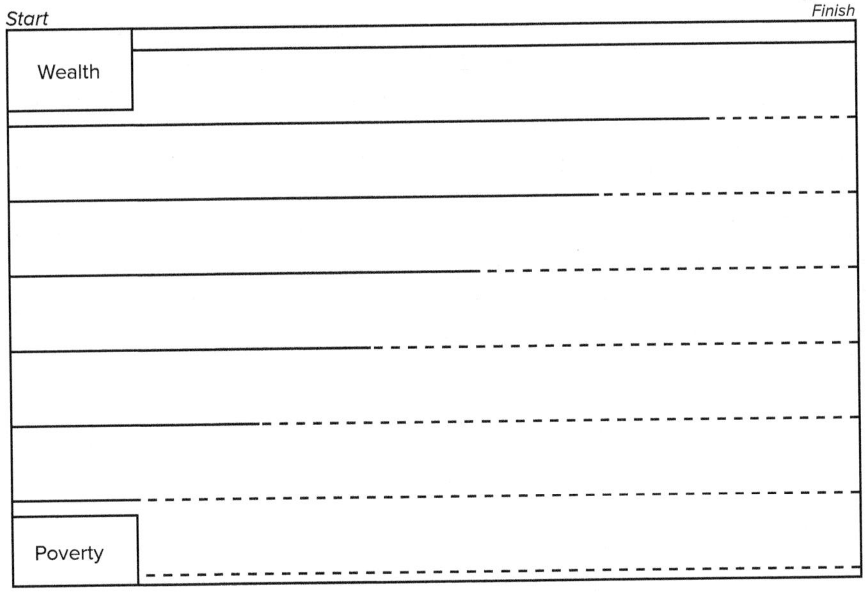

The solid lines represent the effects of inheritance on economic outcomes. The dotted lines represent the potential effects of merit. The "distance" each person needs to reach the finish line on the basis of merit depends on how far from the finish line each person starts the race in the first place.

It is important to point out that equivalent amounts of merit do not lead to equivalent end results. If each dash represents one "unit" of merit, a person born poor who advances one unit on the basis of individual merit over a lifetime ends up at the end of her life one unit ahead of where she started but still at or close to poverty. A person who begins life one unit short of the top can ascend to the top based on an equivalent one unit of merit. Each person is equally meritorious, but his or her end position in the race to get ahead is very different.

Heirs to large fortunes in the world start life at or near the finish line. Barring the unlikely possibility of parental disinheritance, there is virtually no realistic scenario in which they end up destitute — regardless of the extent of their innate talent or individual motivation. Their future is financially secure. They will grow up having the best of everything and having every opportunity money can buy.

Most parents want the best for their children. As a result, most parents try to do everything they can to secure their children's futures. Indeed, that parental desire to provide advantages for children may even have biological origins. Under the "inclusive fitness-maximizing" theory of selection, for instance, beneficiaries are favored in inheritance according to their biological relatedness and reproductive value. Unsurprisingly, research shows that benefactors are much more likely to bequeath estates to surviving spouses and children than to unrelated individuals or institutions (Schwartz 1996; Willenbacher 2003). In a form of what might be called "reverse inheritance," parents may invest in children to secure their own futures in the event that they become unable to take care of themselves. Parents may also invest in their children's future to realize vicarious prestige through the successes of their children, which may, in turn, be seen as a validation of their own genetic endowments or childrearing skills.

Regardless of the source of parental motivation, most parents clearly wish to secure children's futures. To the extent that parents are successful in passing on advantages to children, meritocracy does not operate as the basis for who ends up with what. Despite the ideology of meritocracy, the reality in America, as elsewhere, is inheritance first and merit second. . . .

The Cumulative Advantages Of Wealth Inheritance

Inheritance is more than bulk estates bequeathed to descendants; more broadly defined, it refers to the total impact of initial social-class placement at birth on future life outcomes. Therefore, it is not just the superwealthy who are in a position to pass advantages on to children. Advantages are passed on, in varying degrees, to all of those from relatively privileged backgrounds. Even minor initial advantages may accumulate during the life course. In this way, existing inequalities are reinforced and extended across generations. As Harvard economist John Kenneth Galbraith put it in the opening sentence of his well-known book *The Affluent Society,* "Wealth is not without its advantages and the case to the contrary, although it has often been made, has never proved widely persuasive" (1958, 13). Specifically, the cumulative advantages of wealth inheritance include the following.

Childhood Quality of Life

Children of the privileged enjoy a high standard of living and quality of life regardless of their individual merit or lack of it. For the privileged, this not only includes high-quality food, clothing, and shelter but also extends to luxuries such as entertainment, toys, travel, family vacations, enrichment camps, private lessons, and a host of other indulgences that wealthy parents and even middleclass parents bestow on their children (Lareau 2003). Children do not earn a privileged lifestyle; they inherit and benefit from it long before their parents are deceased.

Knowing with Which Fork to Eat

Cultural capital refers to what one needs to know to function as a member of the various groups to which one belongs. All groups have norms, values, beliefs, ways of life, and codes of conduct that identify the group and define its boundaries. The culture of the group separates insiders from outsiders. Knowing and binding by these cultural codes of conduct is required to maintain one's status as a member in good standing within the group. By growing up in privilege, children of the elite are socialized into elite ways of life. This kind of cultural capital has commonly been referred to as "breeding," "refinement," "social grace," "savoir faire," or simply "class" (meaning upper class). Although less pronounced and rigid than in the past, these distinctions persist into the present. In addition to cultivated tastes in art and music ("highbrow" culture), cultural capital includes, but is not limited to, interpersonal styles and demeanor, manners and etiquette, and vocabulary. Those from more humble backgrounds who aspire to become elites must acquire the cultural cachet to be accepted in elite circle, and this is no easy task. Those born to it, however, have the advantage of acquiring it "naturally" through inheritance, a kind of social osmosis that takes place through childhood socialization (Lareau 2003).

Having Friends in High Places

Everybody knows somebody else. Social capital refers to the "value" of whom you know. For the most part, privileged people know other privileged people, and poor people know other poor people. Another nonmerit advantage inherited by children of the wealthy is a network of connections to people of power and influence. These are not connections that children of the rich shrewdly foster or cultivate on their own. The children of the wealthy travel in high-powered social circles. These connections provide access to power, information, and other resources. The difference between rich and poor is not in knowing people; it is in knowing people in positions of power and influence who can do things for you.

Early Withdrawals on the Family Estate

Children of the privileged do not have to wait until their parents die to inherit assets from them. Inter vivos transfers of funds and "gifts" from parents to children can be substantial, and there is strong evidence suggesting that such transfers account for a greater proportion of intergenerational transfers than lump-sum estates at death (Gale and Scholz 1994). Inter vivos gifts to children provide a means of legally avoiding or reducing estate taxes. In this way, parents can "spend down" their estates during their lives to avoid estate and inheritance taxes upon their deaths. Furthermore, in 2001 the federal government enacted legislation that is scheduled to ultimately phase out the federal estate tax. Many individual states have also reduced or eliminated inheritance taxes. The impact of these changes in tax law on intergenerational transfers is at this point unclear. If tax advantages were the only reasons for inter vivos transfers, we might expect parents to slow down the pace of inter vivos transfers. But it is unlikely that the flow of such transfers will be abruptly curtailed because they serve other functions. Besides tax avoidance, parents also provide inter vivos transfers to children to advance their children's current and future economic interests, especially at critical or milestone stages of the life cycle. These milestone events include going to college, getting married, buying a house, and having children. At each event, there may be a substantial infusion of parental capital – in essence an early withdrawal on the parental estate. One of the most common forms of inter vivos gifts is payment for children's education. A few generations ago, children may have inherited the family farm or the family business. With the rise of the modern corporation and the decline of family farms and businesses, inheritance increasingly takes on more fungible or liquid forms, including cash transfers. Indeed, for many middle-class Americans, education has replaced tangible assets as the primary form by which advantage is passed on between generations.

What Goes Up Doesn't Usually Come Down

If America were truly a meritocracy, we would expect fairly equal amounts of both upward and downward mobility. Mobility studies, however, consistently show much higher rates of upward than downward mobility. There are two key reasons for this. First, most mobility that people have experienced in American in the past century, particularly occupational mobility, was due to industrial expansion and the rise of the general standard of living in society as a whole. Sociologists refer to this type of mobility as "structural mobility," which has more to do with changes in the organization of society than with the merit of individuals. A second reason why upward mobility is more prevalent than downward mobility is that parents and extended family networks insulate children from downward mobility. That is, parents frequently "bail out," or "rescue," their adult children in the event of life crises such as sickness, unemployment, divorce, or other setbacks that might otherwise propel adult children into a downward spiral. In addition to these external circumstances, parents also rescue children from their own failures and weaknesses, including self-destructive behaviors. Parental rescue as a form of inter vivos transfer is not a generally acknowledged or well-studied benefit of inheritance. Indirect evidence of parental rescue may be found in the recent increase in the number of "boomerang" children, adult children who leave home only to return later to live with

PERSONAL ACCOUNT

I Am a Pakistani Woman

I am a Pakistani woman, raised in the U.S. and Canada, and often at odds with the Western standard of beauty.

As a child in Nova Scotia and later growing up in New York and Indiana, I was proud of my uniqueness. On traditional Pakistani and Muslim holidays, I got to wear bright, fun clothes from my country and colorful jewelry. I had a whole rich tradition of my own to celebrate in addition to Christmas and Easter. However, as I started school, I somehow came to realize that being different wasn't so great–that in other people's viewpoint, I looked strange and acted funny. I learned the importance of fitting in and behaving like the other girls. This involved dressing well, giggling a lot, and having a superior, but flirtatious attitude toward boys. I was very outgoing and had very good grades, so outwardly I was able to "assimilate" with some success. But my sister, who was quiet and reticent, often took the brunt of other children's cruelty. I realize how proud and ashamed I was of my heritage when I look at my relationship with my family.

A lesson I learned early on in the U.S. was that being beautiful took a lot of money. It is painful, as an adult, for me to consider the inexorable, never-ending pressure that my father was under to embody the dominant, middle-class cultural expressions of masculinity, as in success at one's job, making a big salary, and owning status symbols. I resented him so much then for being a poor, untenured professor and freelance writer. I wanted designer clothes, dining out at nice restaurants, and a big allowance. Instead, I had a deeply spiritual thinker,

writer, and theologian for a dad. I love(d) him and am so very grateful for what he's taught me, but as a child I didn't think of him as a success.

The prettiest girls in school all had a seemingly endless array of outfits, lots of makeup and perfume, and everything by the "right" designers. I hated my mom for making many of my clothes and buying things on sale (and my mom was a great seamstress). I felt a sense of hopelessness that I could never have the resources or opportunities necessary to compete, to be beautiful.

Instead I found safety in conformity. When I was in high school, the WASPy, preppy look was hot; it represented the epitome of success and privilege in America. I worked hard to purchase a wardrobe of clothes with a polo-horse insignia, by many hours at an after-school job. I tried to hide my exotic look behind Khakis, boat shoes, hair barrettes, and pearl studs. There was comfort in conformity. I saw the class "sex symbol" denigrated for wearing tight dresses and having a very well-developed body for a sixteen-year-old, and the more unique dressers dismissed as frivolous, trendy, and more than a little eccentric. You couldn't be too pretty, too ugly, too different–you had to just blend in.

Though I did it well, I perpetually felt like an imposter. This rigidly controlled, well-dressed preppy going through school with good grades in advanced placement classes in no way represented what I felt to be my true essence.

Hoorie I. Siddique

parents. Social scientists report that 34 percent of young adults are now moving back in with their parents during their twenties (*Contexts* 2008). The reasons for adult children returning to live at home are usually financial: adult children may be between jobs, between marriages, or without other viable means of selfsupport. Such living arrangements are likely to increase during periods of high unemployment, which in early 2009 topped 8 percent of the civilian labor force.

If America operated as a "true" merit system, people would advance solely on the basis of merit and fail when they lacked merit. In many cases however, family resources prevent, or at least reduce, "skidding" among adult children. One of the authors of this book recalls that when he left home as an adult, his parents took him aside and told him that no matter how bad things became for him out there in the world, if he could get to a phone, they would wire him money to come home. This was his insurance against destitution. Fortunately, he has not yet had to take his parents up on their offer, but neither has he forgotten it. Without always being articulated, the point is that this informal familial insurance against downward mobility is available in varying degrees, to all except the poorest of the poor, who simply have resources to provide.

Live Long and Prosper

From womb to tomb, the more affluent one is, the less the risk of injury, illness, and death (Budrys 2003; Cockerham 2000; National Center for Health Statistics 2007; Wermuth 2003). Among the many nonmerit advantages inherited by those from privileged backgrounds is higher life expectancy at birth and a greater chance of better health throughout life. There are several possible reasons for the strong and persistent relationship between socioeconomic status and health. Beginning with fetal development and extending through childhood, increasing evidence points to the effects of "the long reach of early childhood" on adult health (Smith 1999). Prenatal deprivations, more common among the poor, for instance, are associated with later life conditions such as retardation, coronary heart disease, stroke, diabetes and hypertension. Poverty in early childhood is also associated with increased risk of adult diseases. This may be due in part to higher stress levels among the poor. There is also evidence that cumulative wear and tear on the body over time occurs under conditions of repeated high stress. Another reason for the health-wealth connection is that the rich have greater access to quality health care. In America, access to quality health care is still largely for sale to the highest bidder. Under these conditions, prevention and intervention are more widely available to the more affluent. Finally, not only does lack of income lead to poor health, but poor health leads to reduced earnings. That is, if someone is sick or injured, he or she may not be able to work or may have limited earning power.

Overall, the less affluent are at a health disadvantage due to higher exposure to a variety of unhealthy living conditions. As medical sociologist William Cockerham points out,

> Persons living in poverty and reduced socioeconomic circumstances have greater exposure to physical (crowding, poor sanitation, extreme temperatures), chemical and biochemical (diet, pollution, smoking, alcohol, and drug abuse), biological (bacteria, viruses) and psychological (stress) risk factors that produce ill health than more affluent individuals. (1998, 55).

Part of the exposure to health hazards is occupational. According to the Department of Labor, those in the following occupations (listed in order of risk) have the greatest likelihood of being killed on the job: fishers, timber cutters, airplane pilots, structural metal workers, taxicab drivers, construction laborers, roofers, electric power installers, truck drivers, and farm workers. With the exception of airline pilot, all the jobs listed are working-class jobs. Since a person's occupation is strongly affected by family background, the prospects for generally higher occupational health risks are in this sense at least indirectly inherited. Finally, although homicides constitute only a small proportion of all causes of death, it is worth noting that the less affluent are at higher risk for being victims of violent crime, including homicide.

Some additional risk factors are related to individual behaviors, especially smoking, drinking, and drug abuse — all of which are more common among the less affluent. Evidence suggests that these behaviors, while contributing to poorer health among the less affluent, are responsible for only one-third of the "wealth-health gradient" (Smith 1999, 157). These behaviors are also associated with higher psychological as well as physical stress. Indeed, the less affluent are not just at greater risk for physical ailments; research has shown that the less affluent are at significantly higher risk for mental illness as well (Cockerham 2000; Feagin and McKinney 2003). Intriguing new evidence suggests that, apart from material deprivations, part of the link between wealth and health may be related to the psychological stress of relative deprivation, that is, the stress of being at the bottom end of an unequal social pecking order, especially when the dominant ideology attributes being at the bottom to individual deficiencies.

Despite the adage that "money can't buy happiness," social science research has consistently shown that happiness and subjective well-being tend to be related to the amount of income and wealth people possess (Frey and Stutzer 2002; Frank 2007a; Schnittker 2008). This research shows that people living in wealthier (and more democratic) countries tend to be happier and that rates of happiness are sensitive to overall rates of unemployment and inflation. In general, poor people are less happy than others, although increments that exceed average amounts of income only slightly increase levels of happiness. That is, beyond relatively low thresholds, additional increments of income and wealth are not likely to result in additional increments of happiness. Although money may not *guarantee* a long, happy, and healthy life, a fair assessment is that it aids and abets it. . . .

SUMMARY

The United States has high levels of both income and wealth inequality. In terms of the distribution of income and wealth, America is clearly not a middleclass society. Income and especially wealth are not evenly distributed, with a relatively small number of well-off families at one end and a small number of poor families much worse off at the other. Instead, the overall picture is one in which the bulk of the available wealth is concentrated in a narrow range at the very top of the system. In short, the distribution of economic resources in society is not symmetrical and certainly not bell-shaped: the poor who have the least greatly outnumber the rich who have the most. Moreover, in recent decades, by all measures, the rich are getting richer, and the gap between the very rich and everyone else has appreciably increased.

The greater the amount of economic inequality in society, the more difficult it is to move up within the system on the basis of individual merit alone. Indeed, the most important factor in terms of where people will end up in the economic pecking order of society is where they started in the first place. Economic inequality has tremendous inertial force across generations. Instead of a race to get ahead that begins anew with each generation, the race is in reality a relay race in which children inherit different starting points from parents. Inheritance, broadly defined as one's initial starting point in life based on parental position, includes a set of cumulative nonmerit advantages for all except the poorest of the poor. These include enhanced childhood standard of living, differential access to cultural capital, differential access to social networks of power and influence, infusion of parental capital while parents are still alive, greater health and life expectancy, and the inheritance of bulk estates when parents die. . . .

DISCUSSION QUESTIONS

1. On what grounds do McNamee and Miller conclude that America is not a middle-class society? Is their conclusion supportable?
2. In what ways does America function as a meritocracy and in what ways does it not?

REFERENCES

Budrys, Grace. 2003. *Unequal Health: How Inequality Contributes to Health or Illness.* Lanham, MD: Rowman & Littlefield.
Cockerham, William. 1998. *Medical Sociology.* 7th ed. Upper Saddle River, NJ: Prentice Hall.
Feagin, Joe. R., and Mary D. McKinney. 2003. *The Many Costs of Racism.* Lanham, MD: Rowman & Littlefield.
Frey, Bruno S., and Alois Stutzer. 2002. *Happiness and Economics: How the Economy and Institutions Affect Well-being.* Princeton, NJ: Princeton University Press.
Galbraith, John Kenneth. 1958. *The Affluent Society.* New York: Mentor Press.
Gale, William G., and John Karl Scholz. 1994. "Intergenerational Transfers and the Accumulation of Wealth." *Journal of Economic Perspectives* 8: 145-60.
Lareau, Annette. 2003. *Unequal Childhood: Class, Race, and Family Life.* Berkeley: University of California Press.
National Center for Health Statistics. 2007. *Health, United States, 2007, with Chart-book on Trends in the Health of Americans.* Hyattsville, MD: National Center for Health Statistics, U.S. Department of Health and Human Services.
Smith, James P. 1999. "Healthy Bodies and Thick Wallets: The Dual Relation between Health and Economic Status." *Journal of Economic Perspectives* 13: 145-66.
Stephen J. McNamee and Robert K. Miller, Jr., excerpt from "The Silver Spoon: Inheritance and the Staggered Start" from *The Meritocracy Myth,* Second Edition. Copyright © 2009. Reprinted with the permission of Rowman & Littlefield Publishing Group.
Wermuth, Laurie. 2003. *Global Inequality and Human Needs: Health and Illness in an Increasingly Unequal World.* Boston: Allyn Bacon.

PART III

5

HOW TO GET A JOB
OR GET INTO GRADUATE SCHOOL
WHEN YOU GET OUT OF HERE

LISA GREY WHITAKER

Freshman and Sophomore Years

Take IN-PERSON courses in a variety of subject areas. Apply yourself academically. Get the best grades you can in these courses. Go to your instructors' office hours. Ask them about their professional backgrounds and interests. Find at least one instructor you like and cultivate a professional relationship with her or him.

Meet in-person with your academic advisor every semester. Discuss with her or him your academic progress, your career interests at that time and the courses you should be taking during the next semester to move you further toward your goals.

Interact with students from a variety of cultures and backgrounds. Learn about the places they come from, about how people think in those locales and about what their daily lives are like back home. Be open to ways of thinking and doing that are other than those you were raised with. Develop in yourself an ease with face-to-face conversation, with people from all walks of life.

Take 101 through 202 courses in a foreign language. You should choose the language according to what will make you the most marketable in the profession or trade you believe you would like to work in after you graduate. Even if you 'know' you will never need a foreign language for your future career — take those courses anyway.

Work on your ability to express your ideas clearly in writing. If your writing sucks, admit that to yourself and make it a priority to learn to express yourself clearly using correct grammar. Get help from on-campus writing centers or tutoring resources to do this. The ability to produce clean, clear writing is an essential life skill. Make this a priority project for yourself. Do not limit your life chances by blowing it off.

Master the use of basic Microsoft Office programs — Word, Excel and PowerPoint.

Join a student club or organization and actively participate as a member or club officer. Every year, do some form of volunteer work in the community. Every year, hold at least a part-time job, even if only in the summer.

Start building a professional resume and e-Portfolio. Get advice from a professor, academic advisor or career services professional to learn how to prepare these.

Junior Year

You probably have some ideas by now about what you might like to do professionally, after college. If necessary, change your major accordingly.

Complete and/or update your professional resume and e-portfolio.

If you have decided you are interested in an academic career for yourself, approach whichever instructor(s) you have developed a relationship with and ask if it would be possible to get an undergraduate research or teaching assistantship with her or him. If you have an interest in the type of work this instructor does and the instructor can make an assistantship possible for you, be sure to do this during your junior year and/or senior year(s).

If you have become interested in a non-academic career, consult in-person with your academic advisor or with a staff member of the on-campus career services office about off-campus internships that are available in your field of interest. Such internships may take place during the summer before your senior year or during your senior year, itself. Often the competition for such internships is as stiff as for a job; thus you will want to have all your ducks lined up. Go to the instructors, advisors and work supervisors you have a rapport with and get three of them to write you letters of recommendation. Obtain letters from them in both paper and electronic formats. If gaining the internship requires a phone or in-person interview, get a knowledgeable person to prep you for that interview, so you will know the types of questions to expect, how to answer them and how to comport yourself generally.

Think seriously about doing a study-abroad program during either the second semester of your junior year, the summer before your senior year, or the first semester of your senior year. Go physically to the on-campus International Programs Office and learn about study abroad opportunities that interest you. In my experience studying abroad does not cost as much as you might think and there may be scholarship money or some other type of funding to help pay for it. Every time you leave the U.S. to go live in another country for a while, you will grow as a person. You will develop a more cosmopolitan world view. You will become more flexible and adaptable by having to adjust to different culture and way of life. You will become more mature and sophisticated as an individual. You will develop your language skills. You will substantially enhance your marketability as a professional. You will have fun. (!)

Continue to strive to earn the best grades you can in your courses. At this juncture you may need to take some online courses due to your job, internship, assistantship or other extracurricular responsibilities.

Maintain the professional network you have been building by keeping in regular contact with the professors, advisors, peers, work and internship supervisors, and others you have established a rapport with during college. If you do a study abroad, once you return to the U.S., stay in periodic, regular contact with instructors and peers abroad with whom you established rapport while you were overseas. These individuals are now part of your professional network.

During the spring semester of your junior year or the summer before your senior year at the latest, if you are planning to go to graduate school, start researching graduate programs by reviewing their websites. Identify at least three schools you would like to apply to. Research the graduate faculty at the school. Identify one or more faculty member at each school who does research in your area(s) of interest.

Discuss with your professors which graduate programs might be right for you. Ask for and secure letters of recommendation in both electronic and hard-copy format from three professors. Get mentoring on how to write the Personal Statement that is an important part of your application to grad programs. Once you have drafted your Personal Statement, ask one of your professors to read it and give you feedback; then tweak it accordingly.

Senior Year

Preparing for Graduate School

During the fall semester of your senior year, if you are planning to go to grad school, take the GRE, LSAT, MCAT or whatever is the appropriate aptitude test for your field of interest. Apply to grad programs. Email each faculty member in those programs whom you have identified as someone you would like to work with. In your email, explain you are applying to their school's program, that if selected for the program you would like to work with them on their research projects, and tell them why. Tell them what your own research interests are. Explain why you believe you would be a good 'fit' with her/his research team and why you believe that faculty member would make the best mentor for you.

Preparing for Your First Professional Job: Job Fairs

If you are planning to start working right after college, update your resume and professional e-portfolio. Ask members of your professional network to let you know of any job openings they hear about in your field of interest. Remember, most people get their jobs by networking; not by applying for jobs 'cold'. Ask for and secure professional references and/or letters of recommendation from your professors, work/internship supervisors, or practitioners who are already working in your field of interest, with whom you have established a rapport.

Plan to attend multiple job fairs put on by your school and/or in your community. Find out which organizations will be represented at each fair by looking online for a list of companies that will have reps at the event(s) you are attending. If you school is hosting the job fair, its Career Services office will have posted a list of companies on its web page within your school's website.

From the list of organizations that will be in attendance at the job fair, select at least three. Research these organizations via their websites to learn about their current activities, organizational structure, plans for expansion if any, benefit programs for employees, etc. Take notes on what you find so you can study this information before meeting the org representatives.

The 30-Second Biography

Develop your "30-Second Biography" to introduce yourself at the job fair to representatives of companies that interest you. Practice saying it over and over until you've memorized it and can say it easily.

The 30-Second Biography has five components:

1. What your field of interest is and why you chose it
2. Why you chose that organization to contact/interview with; what you know about them
3. What you know about the position the org is hiring for; about the required skills & experience
4. The skills and experience you have that fit what they want
5. Peppy wrap-up statement, e.g. ". . . and I'm really excited about being here/getting the opportunity to talk with you today. . . "

By the way, the 30-Second Bio is also *the* answer to what is often the first question you will be asked in a formal job interview: "Tell me about yourself".

You should prepare for a job fair as seriously as you would prepare for a formal job interview. Why? Because a chat with an org rep at a job fair can *turn into* a job interview before you know it, if a rep likes you.

Therefore, dress for a job fair as you would for a formal interview. Men, wear long-sleeve button-down shirts, ties, and slacks and dress shoes — no jeans, polo shirts, sneakers, etc. Forget about "business-casual". Women, wear suits or a very nice blouse with nice slacks or skirt and modest heels at most. Anyone with long hair should get it back, out of his/her face via barrettes, a pony tail, bun or whatever. Go to the interview squeaky-clean. No excessively strong cologne, after-shave or perfume. With that stuff, less is more.

Make copies of your resume to hand to the reps you talk to. Put them in a folder or small briefcase. You may also want to take your laptop with you, in case it becomes appropriate to show someone your e-portfolio. Boy, will that rep be impressed!

When speaking to the reps at the job fair, be upbeat and outgoing in your demeanor. Put a little spring in your step and a big smile on your face as you approach the reps you have targeted. At the conclusion of your chat with each one, ask her/him for a business card. Ask if you may contact her/him again in the future if you have any additional questions about the company or the position for which they are hiring. Then later, do contact the rep — make her/him part of your growing professional network.

Preparing for Your First Professional Job: Interviewing

Consult with a staff member of your school's Career Services office about how to 'do' a formal job interview. Learn about the types of questions you are likely to be asked. Prepare answers to these in advance and practice saying them over and over. Get a friend to play the role of interviewer and ask you these typical interview questions.

On the day of an interview, get some vigorous exercise beforehand to help you calm down. Then, get squeaky-clean and dress up. Take your laptop with you in case it becomes appropriate to show them all or a portion of your e-portfolio. Arrive at least 10 minutes early for the interview. Remember to smile and put that spring in your step when you greet the interviewer(s)! At the end of the interview, thank the interviewer for the opportunity to speak to her/him. As soon as you get home, type out a thank-you letter to the interviewer and mail it via the US Post Office (no emails!). If you have not heard back from the company as of one week after your interview date, you may call the organization's HR department and inquire about the status of your application.

Academics and Extracurricular Activities

Keep up your grades. Keep in touch with the members of your professional network. If you are doing an internship, be sure to perform your best. Companies frequently hire their interns for 'real' positions. Why would they want to hire someone off the street when they already have someone they know in-house, who they know can do the job and hit the ground running?

Continue to work at least part-time. Continue to do some type of volunteer work in the community. Continue to be active in the school or community clubs and organizations you belong to.

Never burn any bridges. You just never, ever know who could be of assistance to you at some later point in your career development.

sturti/E+/Getty Images

6

HOW TO INTERVIEW FOR A JOB

LISA GREY WHITAKER

The Purpose of a Job Interview

Job interviews are a two-way street: they are a medium for both applicant and employer to get additional information, beyond what has been obtained earlier in the recruitment/application process, about each other.

From the employer's perspective, the purpose of the interview is to evaluate your qualifications and give you more information about the position and the organization. As the interviewee, your purpose is to obtain more information about the position and workplace culture, to help you determine if employment at that organization would be a good 'fit' with your career goals and personality.

The Type of Applicant Employers are Looking For

Employers Are Looking for an Applicant Who:

- Presents a professional image
- Has a healthy self – concept
- Demonstrates maturity through his/her behavior
- Has good interpersonal skills and can interact comfortably with anyone
- Whose personality is a good 'fit' with the organization's workplace culture
- Who is adept at and enjoys teamwork
- Who has a good work ethic
- Who is honest, has integrity and is trustworthy

Additional Qualities Employers Expect from ASU Graduates:

- A certain level of academic performance (the cumulative GPA they are looking for will vary from employer to employer, but they will care about it)
- Demonstrated leadership experience
- Internship experience
- Work experience
- Verbal and written communication skills
- Computer literacy (Word, Excel, Power Point; perhaps more depending on the type of position applied for)

Preparing for the Interview

There are three general categories of activity you should engage in to prepare for an interview: researching the company, doing a self-assessment and preparing yourself to answer the type of questions you are likely to be asked.

Researching the Organization

Read through the information in the company's website. Look at its mission statement and organizational structure. Learn as much as you can about the products and/or services it offers, about its expansion into any new product areas or markets, and about any market trends that apply to the organization.

Through online research and/or informational interviews, find out about its hiring and promotion policies and the predominant management style.

Through online research, obtaining and reading a copy of the company newsletter, doing informational interviews and/or by reading trade journals which contain articles about the organization, learn as much as you can about the workplace culture.

Doing Your Self-Assessment

Keeping in mind the specific skills and experience you must have for the position, according to the official job announcement, articulate for yourself the skills and experience you personally have that match up to these position requirements. Practice describing these out loud to a hypothetical interviewer. Practice either with a friend who role-plays the interviewer, or by looking in a mirror. If you use a friend, (s)he can give you feedback on how you come across. If you look in the mirror, you can give yourself feedback. Practice over and over, until your statements come easily and you can say them with professionalism and confidence.

Be able to prove, by giving specific, concrete and *recent* examples of times when you used them, that you have transferable skills such as problem-solving, decision making, organizing, planning, communication, etc. To do this, identify the examples you will use in the interview and practice saying them out loud. Again, practice either with a friend or by looking in a mirror.

Know what your career goals are and be able to articulate these. Practice saying them out loud.

Know what your work-related values are and, based on your research on the company, assess how good a 'fit' your values are with theirs. If the 'fit' is not good, you should re-evaluate why you are interviewing there. If the 'fit' IS good, then be able to articulate the details of that fit for the employer; it will make you a more desirable candidate in his/her eyes. Practice explaining to the interviewer the ways in which you are a good 'fit' for the position.

Based on your understanding of the organization's workplace culture, assess whether or not that culture is a good 'fit' with your personality. If it is, again, be able to articulate the specifics of that good fit during the interview.

Prepare Your Answers to Common Interview Questions

The type of questions you are likely to be asked during a job interview are called "*behavioral interview questions*". Behavioral interview questions are based on the premise that past behavior is a good predictor of future behavior. Moreover, your *recent* past behavior is a better predictor of your future behavior than is how you behaved in the distant past. Thus, how you handled Situation X last week is a better predictor of how you would handle X next week than is how you handled Situation X five years ago. Accordingly, the interviewer will be looking for answers to her/his questions that describe how you acted *recently*.

To respond to behavioral interview questions you should choose examples from your past experience that are not only as recent as possible, but are also as *relevant* as possible. By relevant, I mean *relevant to the employer's work environment*. Since the interviewer is trying to ascertain how you would handle Situation X in her/his workplace, your examples should come from your work experience, not from your personal life. If you have no prior job experience, then using examples from your college activities/schoolwork would be the next best thing.

Behavioral interview questions usually start with: "Tell me about a time when . . . " or "Give me an example of . . . ". If (s)he feels it is necessary, the interviewer will then probe with additional questions about the experience you have described.

During an interview, you will in all likelihood be asked several behavioral interview questions. Knowing this, you should formulate answers to them and practice giving those responses in front of a friend or in front of a mirror, prior to the actual interview. The following are typical behavioral interview questions.

Frequently Asked Behavioral Interview Questions

1. *Tell me about yourself.* Your answer should consist of the following components:
   - How you chose your field of study/area of professional interest
   - Why you chose that organization to contact/interview with; what you know about them

- What you know about the position you are interviewing for — what you know about the required skills and experience
- Description of the skills and experience you have that fit what the organization is looking for; the type of contribution you can make to the organization if you are hired
- Peppy wrap-up statement, e.g. " . . . and I'm happy to be here/to get the opportunity to talk with you today . . . "

2. ***Why do you want to work here? What makes you a good addition to our team?*** Be sure to have an answer prepared for this type of question because, however they phrase it, you will be asked this. Your answer to this question should consist of: (1) your knowledge of what the company is doing, (2) a statement about specific company activities you would like to be a part of, for example, "I saw on your website that you are expanding into the Asian market and that really excited me, because I would love to work for you overseas", (3) a recitation of the skills and experience you have that match what the employer is seeking and (4) in concrete terms, the type of contribution you will be able to make to the org by using your skills and experience.

   Composing your answer in this way will show the interviewer you did your homework to prepare for the interview. The interviewer will take this as 'evidence' that (a) you're a mature person who knows how to act like a professional and (b) that you must really want to work there, because you took the trouble to really prepare for the interview. All organizations want to hire people who WANT to work there!

3. ***Tell me where you see yourself, five years from now.*** You must respond in a way that tells the interviewer: (1) you will still be working for the same organization in five years, (2) you will have worked your way up the ranks to a certain extent and (3) the type of contribution you will make to the organization. You must NOT talk about expectations for your personal life in five years, or about money/material wealth. You must NOT say anything like, "I expect to have YOUR job in five years" or "I expect to be running the company in five years", etc.

4. ***Tell me about a time you worked with a team.*** You must describe a *specific, concrete* team experience from work or school and the role you played within that team, especially if you were team leader. You must not talk in vague generalities.

5. ***Tell me about a time you were under a lot of pressure and felt a lot of stress.*** You must describe a *specific* stressful situation at work or school and describe how you handled that situation in a constructive manner, such that there was a positive outcome.

6. ***Tell me about a time you had a boss or co-worker you didn't get along with.*** You must describe a *specific, concrete* instance of this at work or school and describe handling that situation in a constructive and professional manner, such that there was a positive outcome. You must demonstrate that you approached the individual directly, suggested you meet over coffee (or whatever) to discuss the situation and tried to work things out between the two of you.

7. ***Tell me about a time you had a problem to solve.*** You must describe a *specific, concrete* work-related or school-related problem (not a personal problem) and describe how you used your maturity, objectivity and logic to bring about a positive solution to the problem. Here, the interviewer is looking for evidence of your analytical abilities and wants to see that you can solve problems by thinking things through rather than flying off the handle; that you are mature and can be objective and logical; that you are *not* immature, emotional and impulsive.

8. ***Tell me about a time when you bent the rules.*** You must describe a *specific, concrete* situation wherein you bent — but did not break — the rules while working at a job, internship or school activity. You must include a statement indicating you told your supervisor what you did *after* (not before) you bent the rules.

9. ***Tell me about a time that you were disappointed by something.*** You must describe a *specific, concrete* disappointment at a work, internship or school situation and describe handling the disappointment in a constructive manner. For example, if you did not get a promotion you were expecting, describe how you went to your boss and asked for guidance as to what you needed to improve on and/or what actions you should take going forward, in order to merit promotion in the future, and that following that conversation you *did* take the steps your employer recommended.

10. ***What kind of salary are you looking for?*** You should answer, "Are you offering me the job?" If the interviewer answers "No", you must respond with something like "Well then, let's talk about that after you offer me the job". If the interview answers "Yes", you must respond by tossing the money-issue back to her/him without mentioning any specific numbers, e.g. "Why don't we wait until you've made me a formal offer before discuss specifics"?

11. ***Do you have any questions for me/us?*** Those questions must be about aspects of the job or organization that you could *not* already have known because you researched the company via its website earlier on. Examples of good questions: "On the average, how many days each month will I be traveling for the job?" "For someone starting in the position I am interviewing for, what is the typical career trajectory?" "Can you tell me something about the team I'll be working with?"

You must NOT ask, "What's the salary for this job?" or ask the interviewer a question that requires her/him to evaluate the org. or people in management in some way, e.g. "What do you like most/least about working here?" or "Is the boss really as much of a jerk as I've heard she is?"

Those types of questions are not appropriate at the interview stage of your job-search process. "What do you like most/least about working here?" is a question you can ask during an informational interview, but not later in the process.

You should never put the interviewer on the spot with a question that requires him/her to 'dish the dirt' on an organization. Too, you should never ask a question at the end of an interview that is something you should already know because you should have researched the company before you even applied for the job.

The Day of the Interview

Calm the Pre-Interview Jitters

The morning of the interview, give yourself a strenuous cardio workout — go to the gym; jog around the neighborhood; whatever. Getting some strenuous physical exercise will lower your blood pressure and in general, help you feel composed for the interview.

Prepare Your Appearance

You must look squeaky-clean, polished and professional. Men should wear a suit or at least a long-sleeve dress shirt, tie, dress slacks (not jeans) and dress shoes. No sneakers or sandals. Women should wear either a suit, business-type dress with jacket, or a professional blouse, nice slacks, and jacket. No low-cut dresses or blouses. No short skirts. No 'party' dresses, 'cocktail' dresses or dresses that look like something you would wear to go 'clubbing.' Your shoes can be dress sandals with a little bit of a heel, or other low-heeled professional shoes. No sneakers or casual, flat-heeled sandals. Whether male or female, get your hair out of your face. Pin it up, pull it back in a ponytail; whatever — just get it out of your face. No gaudy or excessive jewelry. No dangly earrings.

Adjust your Attitude

Psych yourself up to present yourself as someone who has self-confidence and self-assurance; who has a positive outlook on life and is enthusiastic about the prospect of employment with the organization.

Arrive for the Interview

Allow yourself plenty of time to get to the interview. Many organizations will immediately disqualify you as a candidate if you arrive late. They do this because they interpret a late arrival to mean you do not care all that much about working for them. Do what you need to do to arrive for the interview 10-15 minutes early.

As the Interview Begins

Greeting the interviewer

If you are sitting when the interviewer comes out to get you, spring out of your seat to greet him or her. Have a bounce in your step and a big smile on your face. This will be easy for you to accomplish because the adrenalin will be pumping!

Sitting Position

Sit at a slight left angle to the interviewer or interviewers, so that you are making right-eye-to-right-eye contact with each person who asks you a question.

Gaze

In general you should maintain eye contact with your interviewer. That said, if you get a tough question there is nothing wrong with looking away from the interviewer for a moment, to collect your thoughts. Just be sure to *either look up or to one side* while formulating your answer. Never look down at the floor, as this communicates you feel defeated by the question.

Voice Quality

You should sound enthusiastic, upbeat, at-ease. You must avoid using these types of speech:

- "teen speak", e.g. " . . . um, like, you know?" repeated over and over
- any unpleasant (e.g. nasal or strong regional) accent
- a sing-song or interrogative intonation (so that every sentence sounds like a question)

After the Interview

The same day as the interview, type out a hard-copy letter to the person (or to each person if you were interviewed by a panel of persons) who interviewed you. Thank her/him for the talking with you that day. Mention some topic that you and the interviewer discussed — something as unique to you as possible — so that the interviewer will remember you. This is important because the interviewer may have talked to who-knows-how-many applicants the same day and you want her/him to be able to recall you in particular. Mail the letter the same day. Take it to the post office.

One week after the interview, you may call the interviewer or the HR department of the organization to see how the hiring-decision process is progressing. You may call again the week after that, if you still have not heard anything. Remember: companies want to hire people who want to work for them, and calling for updates reflects your ongoing interest in the position.

Design Pics/Carson Ganci

7

HOW TO NEGOTIATE YOUR STARTING SALARY

LISA GREY WHITAKER

Salary negotiation begins when you prepare your resume. Your resume plus your cover letter provide the first items of information the employer gets about you. You have the ability to 'sculpt' the impression the employer has of you by deciding what information to include in your resume and what to omit, etc.

On your resume, you have the ability to convey that you have the skills and experience the employer is looking for. Your resume becomes a handy reference for you later, when you have been offered a position and are about to negotiate salary. Your resume itemizes the skills and experience you bring to the table, which you can pull out — one at a time - and use as bargaining tools later, when you ask for more money than the base salary the employer initially offers you. Specifically, your grades, work experience, internship experience, volunteer experience, extracurricular club/organizational memberships, leadership experience, teamwork experience and multi-cultural experience (travel, studying or working abroad, languages learned, etc.) are all bases for asking for more money.

Early on in the application/recruitment process, the employer may ask you — on a job application form or during an interview — to provide a specific figure for the salary you expect to get. If asked on a form what your salary requirements are, your response should be "negotiable" or "open" or "competitive." If asked in person during an interview, your response should be, "Are you offering me the position?" In all likelihood the interviewer will respond something like, "No, not at this time". Then you say, "Well, let's talk about that when you offer me the job."

Before you enter into salary negotiations, you need to figure out:

1. Whether or not the job you have been offered is a good 'fit' for you in terms of the work per se, the workplace culture, your career goals, etc.
2. The specific elements of your strategy for negotiating a higher starting salary

In any salary negotiations, what you are negotiating is your base salary. The base salary has been referred to as "the gift that keeps on giving." Thus the higher the starting base salary you can get the employer to agree to, the larger your subsequent salaries will be later, as you begin to accrue promotions and raises.

Preparing for Negotiations

- Do your homework — Be able to articulate your strengths and why you are unique; what you can deliver. Figure out your monthly budget — how much money do you really *need* each month to live decently. We all want more money, but you must be realistic. Do research and find evidence that the salary you are asking for is in line with what employees earn who are in similar jobs across the industry. Gain an understanding of the company's employee-evaluation and promotion processes and related salary increases.

- Develop your sales 'pitch' using wording that describes your position in business (professional) terms — what you can do for the organization to help them achieve *their* goals — not in personal terms that relate to your own lifestyle goals. Practice negotiating out loud with a friend who takes the role of the other party.

The Negotiation Itself

- Come to the table with confidence.

- Always start the process with positive comments about the organization and the position.

- Avoid using absolute terms such as *always, never, must have,* etc. Successful negotiation requires moderation. Appearing hard-nosed, impatient or greedy will work against you. Arriving at a figure upon which both sides can agree requires give and take.

- Never be the first to name a specific salary figure. The basic rule of thumb in these negotiations is, "whoever mentions money first, loses."

- If the employer tries to get you to give them a ballpark salary *range*, make sure the bottom figure of the range is the *least* amount of money (as an annual salary) you would accept; what you know you could live on and/or what is commensurate with industry standards. If you provide a range, of course the employer is then going to offer you the figure at the bottom of the range. Well, then you have already been offered the amount that you have determined you can live on . . . and it can only go up from there!

- At this point you should start hauling out your skills and experience, one item at a time, and offer these as reasons you are worth more money. You should be able to get your salary bumped up a few thousand dollars this way.

- Know when to stop the process – be sure that both sides 'win' (come away from the table satisfied they negotiated reasonably and fairly).

- If you are able to agree on a salary during negotiations, great. If you are not, at the least you should thank them and promise to consider their last offer. Then go home, think about it, sleep on it, consult with your friends, etc. Consider your other options.

8

SEXUAL HARASSMENT IN THE WORKPLACE

LISA GREY WHITAKER

Definition of Harassment

Sexual harassment is a form of sexual discrimination and is prohibited by federal and state law. The Equal Employment Opportunity Commission (EEOC) defines sexual harassment as "...offensive, unsolicited and unwelcome conduct of a sexual nature that explicitly or implicitly affects an individual's employment, unreasonably interferes with an individual's work performance or creates an intimidating, hostile, or offensive work environment".

In 1991, a federal court established a "reasonable person" standard for harassment. This means the severity of unsolicited behavior is determined by what a "reasonable person" in the position of the victim would consider offensive. In 1998, the Supreme Court ruled that harassment of homosexuals is also a violation of Title VII of the Civil Rights Act.

Both men and women can be offenders and victims of sexual harassment. Surveys indicate that nearly 90 percent of American women have experienced some type of sexual harassment. Twelve percent of reported sexual harassment cases involve men as victims.

Types of Harassment

Quid pro Quo

"Quid pro Quo" literally means "this for that." In the workplace this typically refers to the trading of sexual favors for specific employment benefits, e.g. a raise or promotion. Here, the focus is on behavior, not the gender of the person doing the behavior.

Creation of a Hostile Work Environment (HWE)

An employee creates a hostile work environment if (s)he says something (e.g. makes sexual jokes or comments) or does something (e.g. shows sexual photos or other visual material, or makes sexual gestures) of a sexual nature that a coworker finds intimidating and/or offensive. A victim of HWE is not obligated to inform the harasser that his/her words or actions are unwelcome. To legally qualify as having created a "hostile work environment," there usually needs to be a documented pattern of such sexually offensive conduct. However, depending on the nature and severity of the conduct, a single incident can be sufficient.

Factors involved in determining whether or not an HWE has been created:

- Is the conduct verbal, physical or both?
- Frequency of the offensive words/actions
- Presence of physical aggression
- Is the alleged harasser a peer or a superior?
- Are others joining in and contributing to the harassment?
- Is more than one victim being targeted by the harasser?

Third-party Harassment

Legally, Person A can be exposed to an offensive remark (and thus a "hostile work environment") merely by walking down the hall and passing by while Person B is harassing Person C. In other words, Person A need not be the intended target of the harassment in order to claim (s)he has been offended.

What to Do If You Are Harassed

If you are a target of sexual harassment, confront the aggressor using the "broken record" technique. The majority of offenders will stop immediately if you follow this procedure.

The "Broken Record" Technique

First, state your position to the offender clearly and repeat it as often as necessary. Tell the harasser her/his attention is unwanted. Don't debate the situation with the offender. Don't assume any responsibility. Don't analyze the harasser's underlying problems. Don't make any references to the harasser's personal life. Be specific, consistent, direct and confident.

Second, prepare a statement in writing about the harasser's actions, your response to them, the time and place the harassment occurred, and the names of any witnesses. If the harasser continues, keep a written record (e.g. journal) of harassment incidents.

Additionally confide in a friend or colleague. Find out if the offender has harassed others. Report the harassment to a supervisor or to HR personnel. If the offender is the supervisor, go to the next level up in authority or follow the company's written policy for handling harassment incidents. File a written complaint.

Individuals who file lawsuits with the EEOC can ask for both compensatory and punitive damages. Anyone who files a lawsuit should have concrete evidence of the harassment to present in court, e.g. witnesses who will testify the harassment occurred.

To Prevail in a Legal Claim:

The victim (i.e. the victim's advocate) must prove that:

- The harassing words or actions were unwelcome and unwanted
- A "reasonable person" would find such conduct offensive
- The harassing words or actions were "sufficiently severe or pervasive to alter the terms and conditions of the victim's employment and create an abusive working environment" . . . This is the criterion for "constructive discharge," which is the legal term for a situation where the suing employee's claim is, "You made me my life (at work) so miserable, I had to quit!" The employee is stating (s)he had to quit because the offender had made the work environment unbearable.

Employer Liability in Harassment Cases

In harassment claims, employers (organizations) as well as individuals can be held liable. An organization/employer is strictly liable for any "quid pro quo" actions of its supervisors/management personnel. An employer is liable for coworker (peer) harassment if (s)he knew about the behavior but did nothing about it.

When a Claim is Filed-the Legal Process

1. An employee files a harassment claim with the EEOC, which has the power to investigate.
2. Mediation ensues, during which the EEOC represents the plaintiff ('victim') and tries to reach a settlement with the company. The company prefers to settle at this level if at all possible, to avoid the costs of going to court.
3. If the company fights the claim, its HR people will write a "position statement," which is a narrative of all the facts + any supporting documentation. They then send the position statement to the EEOC.
4. The EEOC has nine months to evaluate the position statement. If the EEOC determines that there apparently was wrongdoing on the part of the employer, its personnel can enter the organization and start interviewing employees. Assuming those interviews support their initial assessment that there was wrongdoing:
5. The EEOC informs the company it has found sufficient cause to believe the company did something wrong. Arbitration ensues. Arbitration differs from mediation in that once arbitration ensues, no further negotiation is possible. The EEOC offers the company a specific deal (settlement offer), which the company either does or does not accept. If the company does not take the deal that was offered, the alternative is a lawsuit:

6. At this juncture, the EEOC may file a lawsuit against the company on behalf of the victim. In this case, the company is being sued by the federal government. In the alternative, the EEOC may send the victim a "no fault/right to sue" letter. This letter states in effect, "We won't sue on your behalf but you still have right to sue the company yourself." Assuming a lawsuit is filed by the EEOC or by the victim:

7. During the court process, the two sides exchange "discovery" (documentation held by each side is given to the other side, so that each side knows what cards the other side is holding). Each side takes depositions of parties on the other side.

8. If the depositions favor the employer, the company's attorneys will request that the Court enter a "summary judgment." A summary judgment is a court document stating that in the judge's opinion, the lawsuit is frivolous; causing the whole matter to end right there. If the depositions favor the victim:

9. If the depositions support the victim's claim, the matter proceeds to the settlement phase. At this point the employer's attorneys go to the victim's attorneys and say, "what's it going to take to settle this?" At this point, the settlement is going to be a lot larger than it would have been if the company had agreed to settle way back at the mediation stage of the process.

REFERENCES:

Web Sites

U.S. Equal Employment Opportunity Commission: Sexual Harassment www.eeoc.gov/types/sexual_harassment.html

Employers Publications Sexual Harassment Resource www.sexualharassmentpolicy.com

Employer-Employee.com: Your Workplace Information Portal http://www.employer-employee.com

Feminist Majority Foundation Online www.feminist.org/911/harass.html

Books

Gregory, Raymond F., *Unwelcome and Unlawful: Sexual Harassment in the American Workplace*, Ithaca: Cornell University ILR Press, 2004.

Paludi, Michele and Carmen A. Paludi (editors), *Academic and Workplace Sexual Harassment: A Handbook of Cultural, Social Science;* Westport, CT: Praeger Publishers, 2003.

PART IV
Deviance

9

RELATED CONCEPTS AND IDEAS
LISA GREY WHITAKER

Definition of Deviance

In general, sociologists define deviance as behavior that departs from the norm; i.e. departs from whatever standard is typical within a given situation or in Society as a whole. Behavioral departures from the norm can be in either a positive or negative direction (Heckert and Heckert, 2002). We can thus distinguish between 'good' and 'bad' deviance.

Difference between 'Crime' and 'Deviance'

Crime is behavior that has been defined as illegal by the government. The American legal system is predicated on the notion, "nulle poena sine lege" – "no punishment without law." It is equally true that there is no crime without law, because there would be no such thing as crime if no sort of conduct was legally proscribed.

Types of Deviance

An example of positive or *good deviance* would be Olympic gold medalists; whose deviance is their decidedly-superior level of athletic skill, compared to the rest of us. Because they deviate from the norm in a socially-approved, positive direction, we aren't going to arrest these athletes. In fact we give them medals and turn them into celebrities.

Negative or **bad deviance** is behavior that departs from the norm in a way that criticized or condemned by society. Examples of this negative variety range from minimally offensive breaches of etiquette such as cutting in line or picking your nose in public, to supremely unconscionable acts such as the human trafficking or child molesting. When sociologists write or talk about "deviance," you can assume they are talking about bad deviance unless they say otherwise.

Default deviance is not about assessments of behavior. Rather, it pertains to the overall physical functioning of an individual, or any characteristics of appearance, which depart from the average human condition and which the average person would regard as highly undesirable. Significant physical injuries, disabilities or deformities would fall into this category. The word default suggests a lack of something. Here, what is lacking is not only physical normalcy, but also willfulness. That is, the individual's condition is not elective, not willful. It was hardly something(s)he chose to have or make happen; nor is it something (s)he can easily, perhaps ever, remedy. It is not a form of conduct (s)he previously chose to engage in and now can simply stop doing.

Default deviance merits a category in its own right because in our culture we are all so terribly concerned with "fitting in;" with being just like everybody else. And we want to be like everyone else in regard to appearance, at least as much if not more so than in regard to behavior. Thus anyone who is on sight markedly different in appearance from others may be shunned, ignored, stared at, looked through (treated as a non-person), pointed at, laughed at, verbally ridiculed and so on.

When I was twenty-nine I was biking home from work and was broadsided by a drunk driver on a motorcycle. He fled the scene; leaving me sprawled in the middle of the busy thoroughfare. My left calf was pretty much reduced to jello. Miraculously the bone did not break but most of the blood vessels, nerves and muscles were pulverized. Below the knee, my left leg swelled up like a watermelon. My left foot and ankle disappeared. Then the liquid edema turned into a solid, gelatin-like substance. Technically speaking I developed a large "subdural hematoma" inside my calf. I was told to expect amputation.

Once it was determined I would get to keep my leg, I underwent a year of physical therapy to reduce the size of the hematoma and to re-learn how to walk. During that year I dragged my left leg, or rather the watermelon attached to the end of it, around like a ball and chain. Usually a person who saw me for the first time looked horrified for a nanosecond, then shuddered and looked away. I would like to say that it was only small children who pointed at me, laughed and called me names. However my adult coworkers, some of them anyway, did the same thing. Even some of my so-called friends were reticent to be around me during this time.

It was quite a lesson to see how members of this culture stand ever-ready to devalue and ostracize anyone whose physical self appears to be substandard, even when the causes of such 'defects' are completely beyond the individual's control. My experience of default deviance was temporary, in that eventually my leg healed and shrunk back to a normal size. The impression it made on me, of how we stigmatize people with physical differences, endures.

Managing Deviance

Stigma is a discredit, a taint, a stain applied to an individual or to his/her character. The stain may be applied on the basis of some act(s) of wrongdoing, an unwholesome lifestyle, or some radical departure of his/her person or presentation-of-self from Society's conceptions of what is physically or psychologically "normal."

In his writings on stigma, Goffman (1963) distinguishes between already-stigmatized persons and those who have the potential to be stigmatized, if their deviance ever becomes known about. Individuals who have voluntarily disclosed their own deviance, who have had it disclosed by others against their will or who deviate from the norm in a way that cannot be concealed are the discredited. Those whose departures from the norm are concealable and who manage to keep them concealed are the discreditable.

Goffman, Davis (1961) and Turner (1972) have discussed various techniques of stigma management, available to the discreditable and the discredited. *The discreditable* can try to "pass" for normal by employing disidentifiers – props, actions or verbalizations that serve as a smoke screen to cover their deviance. An example of this would be a minister who sermonizes (employs a verbalization) about the evils of adultery as part of a cover-up of his own extramarital affair. The discreditable may also "pass" with the help of others, who are aware of his/her deviance and "cover" for the tainted individual by concealing the truth about his/her past or by helping him/her to construct a cover story, e.g. saying one's relative was traveling abroad when in fact, said relative was in prison.

A different set of techniques is available to *the* already-*discredited,* to help them manage their stigmatization. For one, the discredited can engage in *deviance avowal* – that is, they can raise the subject of their deviance in conversation with a 'normal' person, and then make a joke about it in order to "break the ice." By showing that they can see their own deviance from a 'normal' person's point of view; they are suggesting that they are not so different from the 'normal' person and thus, can be treated as normal for all intents and purposes. Such activities, on the part of the deviant individual, constitute an effort to normalize the way(s) in which (s)he is different from others.

Stigmatized (discredited) individuals can also achieve normalization through the proactive efforts of others. If I have an unconcealable 'watermelon' attached to one of my legs below the knee, as I did after the hit-and-run accident I mentioned earlier, but you politely disattend my deformity when talking to me, you are helping me pretend my deviance does not exist. That is, between us we are establishing a shared reality in which my deformity does not exist. This technique is called *deviance disavowal.*

Sociologists' Views of Deviance

Each sociological perspective has its own view of the 'causes' of deviance and crime and/or of the roles these play in Society. Depending on which perspective they adhere to, sociologists may study one or more of these dimensions of crime and/or deviance: (a) why certain acts are defined as deviant or criminal while others are not, (b) why certain individuals are defined as deviant or criminal while others, who engaged in the same behavior, escape such definition; (c) how individuals learn skills and techniques needed to perform deviant/criminal acts and (d) strategies individuals use to try to explain away or manage deviant or criminal labels they have already been stuck with, or are at risk to be stuck with, should they in fact proceed to do what they are planning to do.

Functionalist Perspective

According to the *functionalists*, under ordinary circumstances there is a consensus among Society's members about what behaviors are good, right and correct and which behaviors are wrong, bad and inappropriate. Behaviors that are significantly bad become "crimes" through legislative action or popular vote. Deviance and crimes are acts that challenge the status quo and thus, threaten the stability of the society. These threats have to be neutralized to preserve the social order. Thus it is good and right to catch and punish the wrong-doers.

One of the founding fathers of Sociology, Emile Durkheim (1897/1951) discussed why citizens break the rules when circumstances arise that are outside the ordinary. For example, during periods of rapid social change such as those brought on by wars, civil unrest or natural disasters, Durkheim hypothesized, it is no longer clear to the average citizen what the rules are, or it appears the rules have been suspended. Such a state of affairs is called anomie, or normlessness. The looting that occurred in New Orleans in 2005, in the wake of Hurricane Katrina, exemplifies this phenomenon.

Functionalists note that public identification and punishment of rule-violators serves a purpose for Society. Specifically, it reminds everybody what the rules are and reinforces the importance of obeying them. It is no accident that criminal court proceedings are open to the public. For those of us who are occupied nine-to-five, the media make sure we are aware of high-profile cases and their dispositions. To the extent the public is made aware of various acts of wrongdoing and the consequences that issue from them, deviance serves a boundary maintenance (Erickson, 1966) or rule-reinforcing function for society.

Conflict Perspective

In contrast, the *conflict view* is that there is not a general consensus among Society's members about what constitutes right and wrong behavior. Thus, your ideas about what is deviant or criminal will depend on what group(s) you belong to; where you sit in the social hierarchy. Those at the top have the wealth, power and/or influence to make the rules for the whole society and to see that those rules are enforced (Quinney, 1975). Because this elite group has the power to do so, they define as deviant or criminal those behaviors that threaten their interests, specifically. From the conflict perspective, the so-called "deviants" of a Society may in fact be its "Robin Hoods;" social protesters or rebels violating the norms on behalf of the little people; ordinary citizens.

To illustrate the conflict view, during the years I worked in the justice system I dealt with a number of "white-collar" criminals. Their crimes often consisted of bilking senior citizens out of their life savings via some large-scale, phony land development scheme. The losses sustained by their victims ranged from hundreds of thousands, to millions of dollars.

These criminals caused far more damage to victims than the average street-level thief, in terms of (a) the sheer number of victims per offender, (b) the amount of the dollar loss per victim and (c) the emotionally and financially vulnerable position the victims were left in. That senior citizen who bags your groceries at the local grocery store may not be working there just to have something to do; (s)he may need the money.

Despite the havoc these criminals wrought in their victims' lives, they rarely got jail time as a sentence. Instead, they were placed on probation. Meanwhile, some guy who was out of work, who had a wife and hungry infant at home, went to jail for stealing baby food and Pampers from a supermarket. This is conflict theory in action.

Both the functionalist and conflict views of deviance and crime are *structural conceptions* in that they identify the cause of rule-breaking as some sort of problem with the system as a whole. In articulating his strain theory of deviance, Robert Merton (1938) discussed what happens when citizens from all levels of society are socialized to want the same "good things of life" — nice house, nice car, good income, etc. — yet all do not get equal access to the means of legitimately (lawfully) attaining those items. He suggested that when denied access to legitimate means of achieving goals, people will find alternative (deviant), perhaps criminal ways to do so.

Other notions of deviance and crime are *process conceptions.* The interactionist conception falls in this category. According to the interactionists, deviance and crime are neither products of some flaw in the overall system, nor are they inherent properties of certain acts. Rather, deviance and crime are precipitates of social interaction.

Interactionist Perspective

Interactionists such as Sutherland and Cressey (1992) have pointed out that the skills and techniques needed to commit certain types of crimes, e.g. safe-cracking, are learned in the same way that any other skills are learned – through interaction, wherein the teachers are usually significant others of the learners.

A number of interactionists, for example Becker (1963) and Goffman (1963), have focused their attentions on the interaction through which certain individuals are labeled, or avoid being labeled as, deviant or criminal. Such interaction is a process of negotiation – negotiation between the alleged wrongdoer and those who have accused him/her of wrongdoing.

Negotiations concerning allegations of deviance or of the perpetration of a crime usually begin when another person – the victim, in the case of a "crime" – sees or hears (or is the target of) something (s)he perceives as wrongdoing. The accused party can offer an alternative account of the behavior in question; thereby suggesting the accusers have misperceived and thus misinterpreted his/her conduct.

Various social and interpersonal factors will of course enter into these negotiations; into the amount of credibility and social clout assigned to each negotiating party. The bargaining chips may be such items as the respective socioeconomic statuses of the offender and the offended-against; age, racial, ethnic or gender differences between accuser(s) and accused; the accused's adroitness at putting a positive spin on the problematic activity; any "attitude problem" the accused appears to have in responding to authority figures and so on.

To give you an example of negotiation leading (or not) to a label, one afternoon I was driving home from work in rush-hour traffic. Vehicles were crawling; bumper to bumper. I was a probation officer at that time and had really had a bad day at work. The traffic congestion was making me crazy. Although I was alone in my vehicle, I decided to move into the carpool lane, where traffic was moving along unhampered by congestion. I looked around and did not see any cops, so I figured I could get away with using the lane illegitimately.

Not 10 seconds after I entered the carpool lane, there were flashing lights behind me. I had to pull over for a highway patrol officer. When he asked for my license, I pulled out the wallet-type object that contained my badge as well as my license. I flipped it open in a way that made sure he would see the badge.

"Oh – what agency are you with?" he asked. I told him where I worked and explained I had had a "really bad day at the office – you know what I mean? A really bad day." I uttered those words in a tone of voice, and with a facial expression, the meaning of which is universal within the law enforcement community. The officer let me off with a, "Well, ok. Just watch it in the future, will ya?" Had I been someone of a different profession, I would have gotten a ticket. In this case my bargaining chips – my profession, badge, facial expression and tone of voice – caused the officer to define me as one of the brethren and thus, served to get me off.

Depending on who prevails in these negotiations, the accused will or won't be stuck with a deviant or criminal label. Even after a label is applied, a tainted individual can still attempt to 'explain' his/her behavior and thereby throw off the yoke of responsibility. The following example from my former employment will serve to illustrate:

One day, while working in the presentence investigations division of the probation department, I was interviewing a defendant who was awaiting sentencing for raping his four-year-old stepdaughter. The DNA and other physical evidence had been consistent with what the little girl told police, such that there was no doubt this individual was the perpetrator. Indeed, he had been found guilty at trial on all counts of the indictment, by jury verdict. When I questioned the defendant about his behavior, he asserted he had unintentionally penetrated this four-year-old one time, and that the little girl herself had caused it to happen. Please note that the quotation marks indicate the offender's exact words:

The defendant explained that his stepdaughter, despite her young age, was just "naturally sexually precocious." All he had been doing was "relaxing" on his double bed one afternoon. As it happened he had just showered, had not yet dressed and had a "full erection" at that time. Right then his stepdaughter entered the room, took one look at his "big dick" and was unable to control herself. She took a flying leap, spread her legs as she descended onto him and thereby impaled herself on his penis.

Sykes and Matza (1957) outline five **techniques of neutralization** an individual can employ, either to legitimate a rule violation (s)he is contemplating, or to justify his/her actions if called to account for them, after the fact. These "techniques" are (1) denial of responsibility (e.g. portraying oneself as a victim of circumstances), (2) condemnation of the condemners (e.g. asserting the prof writes "bad" test questions; plays favorites, etc.), (3) appeal to higher loyalties (pressures to conform to the peer group), (4) denial of injury (e.g., everybody cheats on exams so no one is actually hurt by it) and (5) denial of victim (e.g., asserting "the system" is the real villain of the piece; the rule breaker is only revolting against an unfair policy). During my interview with the child molester, described above, you can see that he was simultaneously portraying himself as a victim of circumstances (denial of responsibility) and claiming the little girl brought the sexual conduct upon herself (denial of victim).

Scott and Lyman (1968) refer to such after-the-fact rationalizations of untoward behavior as accounts, which manifest as either excuses or justifications. *Accounts* are roughly equivalent to Stokes and Hewitt's (1976) aligning actions — verbalizations and/or actions on the part of a rule breaker, to bring his/her conduct into alignment with cultural norms; i.e. to get the behavior publicly defined as non-deviant.

An individual who offers an excuse is admitting to performing the mechanics of the act in question while denying intentionality — that is, denying (s)he intended the result that precipitated from the act. By denying bad intent, (s)he is denying responsibility. ***Excuses*** come in several forms: (a) appeals to accidents ("I know it's due today, but I had my paper stored on my hard drive and my computer crashed"), (b) appeals to defeasibility ("my roommate said he would turn my paper in"), (c) appeals to biological drives ("it's different for men; we have needs") and (d) scapegoating ("I wouldn't have done so bad on the test, but my friend borrowed my notes and never returned them").

An individual who justifies his/her actions admits intentionality, but claims special circumstances existed at that time, which made the act legitimate. ***Justifications*** may come in the form of (a) sad tales ("I was abused as a child") ("so I use drugs now") or (b) quests for self-fulfillment ("Using LSD brings me closer to God").

REFERENCES

Adler, Patricia A. and Peter Adler, "Shifts and Oscillations in Deviant Careers: The Case of Upper-Level Drug Dealers and Smugglers," Social Problems, 31(2) 1983.

Becker, Howard S., Outsiders: Studies in the Sociology of Deviance; Glencoe, IL: Free Press, 1963, pp.1–18.

Davis, Fred; "Deviance Disavowal: The Management of Strained Interaction by the Visibly Handicapped," Social Problems 9:120–132, 1961.

Durkheim, Émile, Suicide: A Study in Sociology; (G. Simpson, ed., J. Spaulding and G. Simpson, trans.), New York: Free Press, 1951 [1897].

Erickson, Kai T., Wayward Puritans: A Study in the Sociology of Deviance; Boston, MA: Allyn and Bacon, 1966

Goffman, Erving; Stigma: Notes on the Management of Spoiled Identity, Englewood Cliffs, NJ: Prentice-Hall, 1963.

Heckert, Alex and Druanna Maria Heckert, "A New Typology of Deviance: Integrating Normative and Reactivist Definitions of Deviance," Deviant Behavior; 23: 449–479, 2002.

Hewitt, John P. and Randall Stokes, "Disclaimers," American Sociological Review 40(1):1–11, 1975.

Merton, Robert K., "Social Structure and Anomie," American Sociological Review 3:672–682, 1938.

Quinney, Richard, Criminology; Boston: Little, Brown, pp.37–41, 1975.

Scott, Marvin, and Stanford Lyman, "Accounts," American Sociological Review 33(1): 46–62, 1968.

Stokes, Randall and John P. Hewitt, "Aligning Actions," American Sociological Review 41(5): 837–849, 1976.

Sutherland, Edwin H., Donald R. Cressey and David F. Luckenbill, Principles of Criminology, 11th Edition; Alta Mira Press, 1992, pp. 88–90

Sykes, Gresham M. and David Matza; "Techniques of Neutralization: A Theory of Delinquency," American Sociological Review; 22:6, pp.664–670, 1957.

Turner, Ralph H.; "Deviance Avowal as Neutralization of Commitment," Social Problems 19 (Winter 1972), pp. 308–321

UpperCut Images/SuperStock

10

THE INFLUENCE OF SITUATIONAL ETHICS ON CHEATING

DONALD L. MCCABE

McCabe uses Sykes and Matza's classic typology of "techniques of neutralization" to classify some of the rationalizations college students use to legitimate their cheating behavior despite the long-standing presence of honor codes at their schools. Based on a survey of over 6,000 students, McCabe shows which neutralization techniques were more commonly used in various familiar situations. Readers will no doubt recognize some of these rationales as they tie their everyday life surroundings to these deviance concepts.

Numerous studies have demonstrated the pervasive nature of cheating among college students (Baird 1980; Haines, Diekhoff, LaBeff, and Clark 1986; Michaels and Miethe 1989; Davis et al. 1992). This research has examined a variety of factors that help explain cheating behavior, but the strength of the relationships between individual factors and cheating has varied considerably from study to study (Tittle and Rowe 1973; Baird 1980; Eisenberger and Shank 1985; Haines et al. 1986; Ward 1986; Michaels and Miethe 1989; Perry, Kane, Bernesser, and Spicker 1990; Ward and Beck 1990).

Although the factors examined in these studies (for example, personal work ethic, gender, self-esteem, rational choice, social learning, deterrence) are clearly important, the work of LaBeff, Clark, Haines, and Diekhoff (1990) suggests that the concept of situational ethics may be particularly helpful in understanding student rationalizations for cheating. Extending the arguments of Norris and Dodder (1979), LaBeff et al. conclude

that students hold qualified guidelines for behavior which are situationally determined. As such, the concept of situational ethics might well describe . . . college cheating [as having] rules for behavior [that] may not be considered rigid but depend on the circumstances involved (1990, p. 191).

LaBeff et al. believe a utilitarian calculus of "the end justifies the means" underlies this reasoning process and "what is wrong in most situations might be considered right or acceptable if the end is defined as appropriate" (1990, p. 191). As argued by Edwards (1967), the situation determines what is right or wrong in this decision-making calculus and also dictates the appropriate principles to be used in guiding and judging behavior.

Sykes and Matza (1957) hypothesize that such rationalizations, that is, "justifications for deviance that are seen as valid by the delinquent but not by the legal system or society at large" (p. 666), are common. However, they challenge conventional wisdom that such rationalizations typically follow deviant behavior as a means of protecting "the individual from self – blame and the blame of others after the act" (p. 666). They develop convincing arguments that these rationalizations may logically precede the deviant behavior and "[d]isapproval from internalized norms and conforming others in the social environment is neutralized, turned back, or deflated in advance. Social controls that serve to check or inhibit deviant motivational patterns are rendered inoperative, and the individual is freed to engage in delinquency without serious damage to his self-image" (pp. 666-667).

Using a sample of 380 undergraduate students at a small southwestern university, LaBeff et al. (1990) attempted to classify techniques employed by students in the neutralization of cheating behavior into the five categories of neutralization proposed by Sykes and Matza (1957); (1) denial of responsibility, (2) condemnation of condemners, (3) appeal to higher loyalties, (4) denial of victim, and (5) denial of injury. Although student responses could easily be classified into three of these techniques, denial of responsibility, appeal to higher loyalties, and condemnation of condemners, LaBeff et al. conclude that "[i]t is unlikely that students will either deny injury or deny the victim since there are no real targets in cheating" (1990, p. 196).

The research described here responds to LaBeff et al. in two ways; first, it answers their call to "test the salience of neutralization . . . in more diverse university environments"(p. 197) and second, it challenges their dismissal of denial of injury and denial of victim as neutralization techniques employed by students in their justification of cheating behavior.

Methodology

The data discussed here were gathered as part of a study of college cheating conducted during the 1990–1991 academic year. A seventy-two-item questionnaire concerning cheating behavior was administered to students at thirty-one highly selective colleges across the country. Surveys were mailed to a minimum of five hundred students at each school and a total of 6,096 completed surveys were returned (38.3 percent response rate). Eighty-eight percent of the respondents were seniors, nine percent were juniors, and the remaining three percent could not be classified. Survey administration emphasized voluntary participation and assurances of anonymity to help combat issues of non-response bias and the need to accept responses without the chance to question or contest them.

The final sample included 61.2 percent females (which reflects the inclusion of five all – female schools in the sample and a slightly higher return rate among female students) and 95.4 percent U.S. citizens. The sample paralleled the ethnic diversity of the participating schools (85.5 percent Anglo, 7.2 percent Asian, 2.6 percent African American, 2.2 percent Hispanic and 2.5 percent other); their religious diversity (including a large percentage of students who claimed no religious preference, 27.1 percent); and their mix of undergraduate majors (36.0 percent humanities, 28.8 percent social sciences, 26.8 percent natural sciences and engineering, 4.5 percent business, and 3.9 percent other).

Results

Of the 6,096 students participating in this research, over two-thirds (67.4 percent) indicated that they had cheated on a test or major assignment at least once while an undergraduate. This cheating took a variety of different forms, but among the most popular (listed in decreasing order of mention) were: (1) a failure to footnote sources in written work, (2) collaboration on assignments when the instructor specifically asked for individual work, (3) copying from other students on tests and examinations, (4) fabrication of bibliographies, (5) helping someone else cheat on a test, and (6) using unfair methods to learn the content of a test ahead of time. Almost one in five students (19.1 percent) could be classified as active cheaters (five or more self – reported incidents of cheating). This is double the rate reported by LaBeff et al. (1990), but they asked students to report only cheating incidents that had taken place in the last six months. Students in this research were asked to report all cheating in which they had engaged while an undergraduate – a period of three years for most respondents at the time of this survey.

Students admitting to any cheating activity were asked to rate the importance of several specific factors that might have influenced their decisions to cheat. These data establish the importance of denial of responsibility and condemnation of condemners as neutralization techniques. For example, 52.4 percent of the respondents who admitted to cheating rated the pressure to get good grades as an important influence in their decision to cheat, with parental pressures and competition to gain admission into professional schools singled out as the primary grade pressures. Forty-six percent of those who had engaged in cheating cited excessive workloads and an inability to keep up with assignments as important factors in their decisions to cheat.

In addition to rating the importance of such preselected factors, 426 respondents (11.0 percent of the admitted cheaters) offered their own justifications for cheating in response to an open-ended question on motivations for cheating. These responses confirm the importance of denial of responsibility and condemnation of condemners as neutralization techniques. They also support LaBeff et al.'s (1990) claim that appeal to higher loyalties is an important neutralization technique. However, these responses also suggest that LaBeff et al.'s dismissal of denial of injury as a justification for student cheating is arguable.

As shown in the table, denial of responsibility was the technique most frequently cited (216 responses, 61.0 percent of the total) in the 354 responses classified into one of Sykes and Matza's five categories of neutralization. The most common responses in this category were mind block, no understanding of the material, a fear of failing, and unclear explanations of assignments. (Although it is possible that some instances of mind block and a fear of failing included in this summary would be more accurately classified as rationalization, the wording of all responses included here suggests that rationalization preceded

Neutralization Strategies: Self-Admitted Cheaters

Strategy	Number	Percent
Denial of responsibility	216	61.0
Mind block	90	25.4
No understanding of material	31	8.8
Other	95	26.8
Condemnation of condemners	99	28.0
Pointless assignment	35	9.9
No respect for professor	28	7.9
Other	35	10.2
Appeal to higher loyalties	24	6.8
Help a friend	10	2.8
Peer pressure	9	2.5
Other	5	1.5
Denial of injury	15	4.2
Cheating is harmless	9	2.5
Does not matter	6	1.7

the cheating incident. Responses that seem to involve post hoc rationalizations were excluded from this summary.) Condemnation of condemners was the second most popular neutralization technique observed (99 responses, 28.0 percent) and included such explanations as pointless assignments, lack of respect for individual professors, unfair tests, parents' expectations, and unfair professors. Twenty-four respondents (6.8 percent) appealed to higher loyalties to explain their behavior. In particular, helping a friend and responding to peer pressures were influences some students could not ignore. Finally fifteen students (4.2 percent) provided responses that clearly fit into the category of denial of injury. These students dismissed their cheating asharmless since it did not hurt anyone or they felt cheating did not matter in some cases (for example, where an assignment counted for a small percentage of the total course grade).

Detailed examination of selected student responses provides additional insight into the neutralization strategies they employ.

Denial of Responsibility

Denial of responsibility invokes the claim that the act was "due to forces outside of the individual and beyond his control such as unloving parents" (Sykes and Matza 1957, p. 667). For example, many students cite an unreasonable workload and the difficulty of keeping up a sample justification for cheating:

> Here at . . . , you must cheat to stay alive. There's so much work and the quality of materials from which to learn, books, professors, is so bad that there's no other choice.
> It's the only way to keep up.
> I couldn't do the work myself.

The following descriptions of student cheating confirm fear of failure is also an important form of denial of responsibility:

> . . . a take-home exam in a class I was failing
> . . . was near failing.

Some justified their cheating by citing the behavior of peers:

> Everyone has test files in fraternities, etc. If you don't, you're at a great disadvantage.
> When most of the class is cheating on a difficult exam and they will ruin the curve, it influences you to cheat so your grade won't be affected.

All of these responses contain the essence of denial of responsibility: the cheater has deflected blame to others or to a specific situational context.

Denial of Injury

As noted in the table, denial of injury was identified as a neutralization technique employed by some respondents. A key element in denial of injury is whether one feels "anyone has clearly been hurt by [the] deviance." In invoking this defense, a cheater would argue "that his behavior does not really cause any great harm despite the fact that it runs counter to the law" (Sykes and Matza 1957, pp. 667–668). For example, a number of students argued that the assignment or test on which they cheated was so trivial that no one was really hurt by their cheating.

> These grades aren't worth much therefore my copying doesn't mean very much. I am ashamed, but I'd probably do it the same way again.

> If I extend the time on a take – home it is because I feel everyone does and the teacher kind of expects it. No one gets hurt.

As suggested earlier, these responses suggest the conclusion of LaBeff et al. that "[i]t is unlikely that students will . . . deny injury" (1990, p. 196) must be re-evaluated.

The Denial of the Victim

LaBeff et al. failed to find any evidence of denial of the victim in their student accounts. Although the student motivations for cheating summarized in the table support this conclusion, at least four students (0.1% of the self-admitted cheaters in this study) provided comments elsewhere on the survey instrument which involved denial of the victim. The common element in these responses was a victim deserving of the consequences of the cheating behavior and cheating was viewed as "a form of rightful retaliation or punishment"(Sykes and Matza 1957, p. 668).

> This feeling was extreme in one case, as suggested by the following student who felt her cheating was justified by the

> realization that this school is a manifestation of the bureaucratic capitalist system that systematically keeps the lower classes down, and that adhering to their rules was simply perpetuating the institution.

This "we" versus "they" mentality was raised by many students, but typically in comments about the policing of academic honesty rather than as justification for one's own cheating behavior. When used to justify cheating, the target was almost always an individual teacher rather than the institution and could be more accurately classified as a strategy ofcondemnation of condemners rather than denial of the victim.

The Condemnation of Condemners

Sykes and Matza describe the condemnation of condemners as an attempt to shift "the focus of attention from [one's] own deviant acts to the motives and behavior of those who disapprove of [the] violations. [B]y attacking others, the wrongfulness of [one's] own behavior is more easily repressed or lost to view" (1957, p. 668). The logic of this strategy for student cheaters focused on issues of favoritism and fairness. Students invoking this rationale describe "uncaring, unprofessional instructors with negative attitudes who were negligent in their behavior" (LaBeff et al. 1990, p. 195). For example:

> In one instance, nothing was done by a professor because the student was a hockey player.

> The TAs who graded essays were unduly harsh.

> It is known by students that certain professors are more lenient to certain types, e.g., blondes or hockey players.

> I would guess that 90% of the students here have seen athletes and/or fraternity members cheating on an exam or papers. If you turn in one of these culprits, and I have, the penalty is a five-minute lecture from a coach and/or administrator. All these add up to a "who cares, they'll never do anything to you anyway" attitude here about cheating.

> Concerns about the larger society were an important issue for some students:

> When community frowns upon dishonesty, then people will change.

> If our leaders can commit heinous acts and then lie before Senate committees about their total ignorance and innocence, *then why can't I cheat a little?*

> In today's world you do anything to be above the competition.

In general, students found ready targets on which to blame their behavior and condemnation of the condemners was a popular neutralization strategy.

The Appeal to Higher Loyalties

The appeal to higher loyalties involves neutralizing "internal and external controls . . . bysacrificing the demands of the larger society for the demands of the smaller social groups to which the [offender] belongs. [D]eviation from certain norms may occur not because the norms are rejected but because other norms, held to be more pressing or involving a higher loyalty, are accorded precedence" (Sykes and Matza 1957, p. 669). For example, a difficult conflict for some students is balancing the desire to help a friend against the institution's rules on cheating. The student may not challenge the rules, but rather views the need to help a friend, fellow fraternity/sorority member, or roommate to be a greater obligation which justifies the cheating behavior.

Fraternities and sororities were singled out as a network where such behavior occurs with some frequency. For example, a female student at a small university in New England observed:

> There's a lot of cheating within the Greek system. Of all the cheating I've seen, it's often been men and women in fraternities and sororities who exchange information or cheat.

The appeal to higher loyalties was particularly evident in student reactions concerning the reporting of cheating violations. Although fourteen of the thirty-one schools participating in this research had explicit honor codes that generally require students to report cheating violations they observe, less than one-third (32.3 percent) indicated that they were likely to do so. When asked if they would report a friend, only 4 percent said they would and most students felt that they should not be expected to do so. Typical student comments included:

> Students should not be sitting in judgment of their own peers.
> The university is not a police state.

For some this decision was very practical:

> A lot of students, 50 percent, wouldn't because they know they will probably cheat at some time themselves.

For others, the decision would depend on the severity of the violation they observed and many would not report what they consider to be minor violations, even those explicitly covered by the school's honor code or policies on academic honesty. Explicit examination or test cheating was one of the few violations where students exhibited any consensus concerning the need to report violations. Yet even in this case many students felt other factors must be considered. For example, a senior at a woman's college in the Northeast commented:

> It would depend on the circumstances. If someone was hurt, *very likely*. If there was no single victim in the case, if the victim was [the] institution . . . , then *very unlikely*.

Additional evidence of the strength of the appeal to higher loyalties as a neutralization technique is found in the fact that almost one in five respondents (17.8 percent) reported that they had helped someone cheat on an examination or major test. The percentage who have helped others cheat on papers and other assignments is likely much higher. Twenty-six percent of those students who helped someone else cheat on a test reported that they had never cheated on a test themselves, adding support to the argument that peer pressure to help friends is quite strong.

Conclusions

From this research it is clear that college students use a variety of neutralization techniques to rationalize their cheating behavior, deflecting blame to others and/or the situational context, and the framework of Sykes and Matza (1957) seems well-supported when student explanations of cheating behavior are analyzed. Unlike prior research (LaBeff et al. 1990), however, the present findings suggest that students employ all of the techniques described by Sykes and Matza, including denial of injury and denial of victim. Although there was very limited evidence of the use of denial of victim, denial of injury was not uncommon. Many students felt that some forms of cheating were victimless crimes, particularly on assignments that accounted for a small percentage of the total course grade. The present research does affirm LaBeff et al.'s finding that denial of responsibility and condemnation of condemners are the neutralization techniques most frequently utilized by college students.Appeal to higher loyalties is particularly evident in neutralizing institutional expectations that students report cheating violations they observe.

The present results clearly extend the findings of LaBeff et al. into a much wider range of contexts as this research ultimately involved 6,096 students at thirty-one geographically dispersed institutions ranging from small liberal arts colleges in the Northeast to nationally prominent research universities in the South and West. Fourteen of the thirty-one institutions have long — standing honor — code traditions. The code tradition at five of these schools dates to the late 1800s and all fourteen have codes that survived the student unrest of the 1960s. In such a context, the strength of the appeal to higher loyalties and the denial of responsibility as justifications for cheating is a very persuasive argument that neutralization techniques are salient to today's college student. More importantly, it may suggest fruitful areas of future discourse between faculty, administrators, and students on the question of academic honesty.*

REFERENCES

Baird, John S. 1980. "Current Trends in College Cheating." *Psychology in Schools* 17: 512–522.

Davis, Stephen E, Cathy A. Grover, Angela H. Becker, and Loretta N. McGregor. 1992. "Academic Dishonesty: Prevalence, Determinants, Techniques, and Punishments." *Teaching of Psychology*. In press.

Edwards, Paul. 1967. *The Encyclopedia of Philosophy*, no, 3, Paul Edwards (ed.), New York: Macmillan Company and Free Press.

Eisenberger, Robert, and Dolores M. Shank. 1985. "Personal Work Ethic and Effort Training Affect Cheating." *Journal of Personality and Social Psychology* 49: 520–528.

Haines, Valerie J., George Diekhoff, Emily LaBeff, and Robert Clark. 1986. "College Cheating: Immaturity, Lack of Commitment, and the Neutralizing Attitude." *Research in Higher Education* 25: 342–354.

LaBeff, Emily E., Robert E. Clark, Valerie J. Haines, and George M. Diekhoff. 1990. "Situational Ethics and College Student Cheating." *Sociological Inquiry* 60: 190–198.

Michaels, James W., and Terance Miethe. 1989. "Applying Theories of Deviance to Academic Cheating." *Social Science Quarterly* 70: 870–885.

Norris, Terry D., and Richard A. Dodder. 1979. "A Behavioral Continuum Synthesizing Neutralization Theory, Situational Ethics and Juvenile Delinquency." *Adolescence* 55: 545–555.

Perry, Anthony R., Kevin M. Kane, Kevin J. Bernesser, and Paul T. Spicker. 1990. "Type A Behavior, Competitive Achievement-Striving, and Cheating Among College Students." *Psychological Reports* 66: 459–465.

Sykes, Gresham M., and David Matza. 1957. "Techniques of Neutralization: A Theory of Delinquency."*American Sociological Review* 22: 664–670.

Tittle, Charles, and Alan Rowe. 1973. "Moral Appeal, Sanction Threat, and Deviance: An Experimental Test." *Social Problems* 20: 488–498.

Ward, David. 1986. "Self-Esteem and Dishonest Behavior Revisited." *Journal of Social Psychology* 123: 709–713.Ward, David, and Wendy L. Beck. 1990. "Gender and Dishonesty." *Journal of Social Psychology* 130: 333–339.

*The author would like to acknowledge the support of the Rutgers Graduate School of Management Research Resources Committee, Exxon Corporation, and First Fidelity Bancorporation.
The Influence of Situational Ethics on Cheating Among College Students" by Donald I. McCabe, from Sociological Inquiry, 62:3, pp. 365–74. Copyright © 1992 Alpha Kappa Delta: The International Sociological Honor Society. Reproduced by permission of Blackwell Publishing Ltd.

PART V
Relationships

11

CLOSE TIES
RELATED CONCEPTS AND IDEAS
LISA GREY WHITAKER

Friendship

Fehr (1996, p. 7) has defined friendship as "a voluntary, personal relationship, typically providing intimacy and assistance, in which the two parties like each other and seek each other's company." While certainly that's accurate, I prefer the definition I saw once in a greeting card: "Friends are the family we choose for ourselves."

How do you make friends with another person? What factors are involved? Research by Hays (1985) suggests that first-year college students form friendships on the basis of residential proximity, availability (a meshing of daily schedules) and the degree of shyness or outgoingness of the individuals involved.

More generally, a number of factors are involved. First, individuals differ in the type of friendship they want; depending on whether they are **high** or **low self-monitors** (Miller, Perlman and Brehm, 2007, p. 237). High self-monitors seek broad networks of friends with whom they share interests and participation in specific activities, but not much else. Low self-monitors have fewer friends but have more in common with, and get closer to, each of them.

In developing a friendship with somebody, **proximity** initially weighs in. The pool of individuals available to make friends **with** is delimited to a certain extent by geography–who you live near, who you have classes with, who you work with, who your friends and relatives introduce you to. **Mere exposure**-the effect of encountering someone over and over, on a regular basis-facilitates friendship development. These days, of course, you can also meet people via the internet-but it won't be unless-and-until you meet them in person that you will know for sure whether or not they are who they have portrayed themselves to be.

The next filter someone destined to be your friend must pass through is **responsiveness**. You are more likely to perceive, as friendship material, those who respond positively to your words and actions-i.e., those who respond with interest, appreciation of your sense of humor, agreement with your point of view, etc-than those whose responses are lukewarm or negative.

At some point you will have interacted with a friend-prospect enough to have a sense of how similar his/her values, opinions, attitudes, world view, etc. are to yours. Assuming the two of you do are in sync at that level, you will have found someone who validates your own views of things. It appears that merely the **rewards of interaction** (Berscheid and Walster, 1978; Burleson, 1994) with a similar other makes friendship development more likely.

All that said, you might encounter the greatest friend-prospect in the world, but at a time when you simply do not have the time and energy it takes to develop a new friendship with anyone. If your **friendship budget** does not at the time permit expenditure of the requisite amount of time and energy to develop a new friend, you may not do so.

General attributes of friendship include: equality, acceptance, respect, loyalty, responsiveness, support, commitment and **capitalization**; i.e. getting excited about your friend's successes and celebrating them. College students (Hays, op. cit.) judged how close of a friend someone was by the degree to which their friendship with that person provided companionship (sharing activities), consideration (providing help and support), communication (in particular, self-disclosure) and affection.

Argyle and Henderson (1985) did a cross-cultural study on friendship norms. They enumerated a large set of expectations that friends might have of each other; then asked citizens of England, Italy, Hong Kong and Japan which ones seemed most valid. Based on the responses they received, they concluded these rules of friendship were universal:

- Volunteer help in time of need
- Respect the friend's privacy
- Keep confidences
- Trust and confide in each other
- Stand up for the other person in their absence
- Don't criticize each other in public
- Show emotional support
- Look him/her in the eye during conversation
- Strive to make him/her happy while in the other's company
- Don't be jealous or critical of each other's relationships
- Be tolerant of each other's friends
- Share news of success with the other
- Ask for personal advice
- Don't nag
- Engage in joking or teasing with the friend
- Seek to repay debts and favors and compliments
- Disclose personal feelings or problems to the friend

How does this list compare to American cultural norms regarding friendship?

In general, one could say that friendships and romantic relationships differ in emotional intensity, degree of exclusivity, (presence or absence of) sexual intimacy and stringency of standards of conduct. Muddying the waters a little is the phenomenon of friendships "with benefits;" popularized in the mid-90's by Alanis Morrissette in her song, "Head over Feet." *Friends with benefits* are two people who consider themselves good friends, who additionally have sex. They engage in sex for fun and/or to get their sexual needs met, without any intention of entering into a monogamous, committed relationship.

What factors contributed to the friends-with-benefits phenomenon? Why has this type of relationship become popular? One could argue it is an efficient way to meet one's sexual needs, for those who don't have the time and energy to invest in a conventional relationship, or simply aren't interested in one. For some, the no-strings-attached nature of the relationship may provide a sense of security–involvement in a relationship without expectations of exclusivity may obviate the prospect of feeling hurt or rejected if the relationship should end.

Dating

Q: What do most people do on a date?
- A: Dates are for having fun, and people should use them to get to know each other. Even boys have something to say if you listen long enough. (Lynnette, age 8)
- A: On the first date, they just tell each other lies and that usually gets them interested enough to go for a second date. (Martin, age 10)

Q: What would you do on a first date that was turning sour?
- A: I'd run home and play dead. The next day I would call all the newspapers and make sure they wrote about me in all the dead columns. (Craig, age 9)

Q: When is it okay to kiss someone?

- • A: When they're rich. (Pam, age 7)
- • A: The law says you have to be eighteen, so I wouldn't want to mess with that. (Curt, age 7)

Dating emerged in the early 20th century as a distinctly-American phenomenon. A variety of factors were catalysts for its development: the Industrial Revolution and accompanying rural-to-urban migration; the invention of the telephone; the increase in the number of free, public, coed high schools; women's entry into the work force as of WWI and the invention of the automobile, to name a few.

As of WWI, dating was relatively structured–men did the asking, activity-planning and paying. By WWII, the phenomenon of "steady dating"–dating one person exclusively–emerged and served to bridge the gap between casual dating and engagement.

Toward the end of the 20th century, opportunities for even more casual relationships increased; spurred in part by the increasing prevalence of coed housing and increasingly equal enrollment in degree programs which, historically, had for the most part been populated by one sex or other. The structured pattern of relationship-development (dating → going steady → "pinning" → engagement → marriage) disintegrated (DeGenova, 2007, pp. 117–118).

If you are dating someone exclusively, you expect her/him to comply with certain monogamous-relationship norms. When Baxter (1986) studied the breakups of college-age (monogamous, dating) couples, she found that failing to meet your boyfriend's or girlfriend's expectations in any of these eight areas placed you at risk to be 'dumped':

Relationship Area:	Norm Violation:
Autonomy	Possessiveness, smothering
Similarity	Different or conflicting values, interests, attitudes
Supportiveness	Criticism, thoughtlessness, lack of consideration
Openness	Guardedness, secrecy
Fidelity	Cheating
Togetherness	Avoidance, rationing of accessibility
Equity	Selfishness, dominance, exploitation
Romance ("Magic")	Routinization of the relationship, lack of spontaneity, special treats or surprises

Some (e.g. Harris, 2003), feel the U.S. dating system is undesirable for these reasons: It is based on romantic attraction (more volatile) rather than friendship (more stabilizing). Dating couples may mistake sex for love and/or see love and romance as solely recreational pursuits. Dating takes young adults' time and energy away from other important relationships (with close friends and family) and from essential pursuits (preparing for their futures). What do you think?

These days, you have the option of ***hooking up***–meeting someone, finding there is 'chemistry' between the two of you, and proceeding to some degree of a sexual encounter (anything from kissing to intercourse), without emotional involvement or future expectations. In your view, what are the pros and cons of this option?

Mate Selection

Q: Is it better to be single or married?

- • A: I don't know which is better, but I'll tell you one thing. I'm never going to have sex with my wife. I don't want to be all grossed out. (Theodore, age 8)

Q: How do you decide who to marry?

- • A: You got to find somebody who likes the same stuff. Like, if you like sports, she should like it that you like sports and she should keep the chips and dip coming. (Alan, age 10)

- A: No person really decides before they grow up who they're going to marry. God decides it all way before, and you get to find out later who you're stuck with. (Kirsten, age 10)

Q: What is the right age to get married?

- A: Twenty-three is the best age because you know the person FOREVER by then. (Camille, age 10)
- A: No age is good to get married at. You got to be a fool to get married. (Freddie, age 6)

Q: How can a stranger tell if two people are married?

- A: You might have to guess, based on whether they seem to be yelling at the same kids. (Derrick, age 8)

Q: How would the world be different if people didn't get married?

- A: There sure would be a lot of kids to explain, wouldn't there? (Kelvin, age 8)

For those who choose to get married, mate selection is a filtering process. You gradually weed out unsuitable others by applying an increasingly stringent set of standards to your pool of eligibles.

As with developing a friendship, in mate selection the first criterion (filter) you will apply is **proximity**. Next you will narrow the field according to **attraction**; selecting out those whose looks, personality and social characteristics (ethnicity, education, socioeconomic status, religion, etc.) are what you are looking for. Most people make these decisions based on **homogamy**-focusing on persons who are similar to oneself in social characteristics and perceived attractiveness. Others, however, seek mates on the basis of **heterogamy**; focusing on persons who are different from themselves in those areas.

Once you have an established girlfriend or boyfriend, you assess that person's **compatibility**-the degree to which her/his temperament, needs, habits, values, etc. are a good 'fit' with your own. Family members may be pressuring you to go in the direction of **endogamy**; marrying someone within your 'group,' be it a religious, ethnic, or social class grouping. In some cultures, family members apply the opposite sort of pressure-to get the individual to marry outside of his/her social group (**exogamy**). As a final test of compatibility, you may decide go through a period of engagement, and/or try living with your prospective spouse for awhile, before deciding for certain to marry.

Love

Ann Landers characterized love as "friendship that has caught fire" (1982, p. 12). All of us at one time or another have probably mistaken sexual craving for love. However, lust by itself isn't love; it's just (as Landers put it) " . . . one set of glands calling to another (p. 2)."

During the 1998 *ABC News 20/20* program, "Love, Lust and Marriage: Why We Stay and Why We Stray," host John Stossel discusses with guests the notion that lasting love progresses through three stages: lust (sexual craving), infatuation (thinking about the person all the time; can't wait to talk to them on the phone or see them, etc.) and attachment (your life has become so intertwined with your mate's that you cannot imagine life *without* her or him). Sternberg (1987) suggests the type of love that is viable over time has three components: emotional intimacy, passion and commitment. Emotional intimacy entails communication, warmth, understanding, support and sharing. The passion component may have to do with sexual passion, *or* with other strong emotional needs that you and your partner fulfill for each other. Commitment refers to your decision to devote yourself to the relationship and to work to maintain it.

Couple 'Styles'

McCarthy and McCarthy (2004) discuss four common marital 'styles' for couples-complimentary, conflict minimizing, best friend and emotionally expressive. These conceptualizations, of how couple-members relate to each other, seem useful for describing established but unmarried couples, as well.

The **complimentary** couple style is the most popular style, because it blends autonomy and coupleness. There is less emotional closeness than the *best friend* style, but that is preferred. The couple members have and value their autonomy and have the freedom to pursue their individual interests. Each has his/her own domains of competence and influence. A major strength is each member's contribution. The communication pattern is asking about each other's day and experiences, listening, providing emotional support and offering help when asked. The focus is on working together and maintaining a compatible, functional relationship. Arguments and conflicts are addressed and dealt with, as both parties are eager to reach understandings and agreements. Sex is positive and functional, but is not made into a 'big production.' The dangers that accompany this style are that the relationship may become routine and stagnant; roles each member plays may become rigid, and the parties may grow apart and feel less involved in each other's lives.

The *conflict-minimizing* couple style is the most stable. These couples often follow traditional religious and gender norms so that there is less conflict, less need for negotiation. Communication is supportive and non-adversarial. Such couples maintain strong personal boundaries. They share activities with other couples and families; the extended family in particular. Affection and sex are valued within the confines of traditional roles. The biggest trap for these couples is that some problems and conflicts are substantial and cannot be avoided and when they occur, these couples are not equipped to handle them. They have been so intent on avoiding problems; just smoothing things over, that by the time a problem can no longer be avoided and must be addressed, disaster may be looming or a problem may have become chronic. Personal growth is inhibited to the extent the parties fear that *any* form of change could damage the relationship. To keep such relationships viable, the couple must guard against complacency, stay vigilant as to the health of the relationship and address problems openly and in a timely fashion.

At its core, the relationship of a **best friend** couple is a trusting, respectful, best-friendship. The couple shares numerous interests and activities as well as household chores. They deal with problems and conflicts frankly, constructively and without delay. Sex is creative. Each partner is free to initiate sex and make requests. Potential traps for these couples are: losing autonomy and individuality for the sake of 'coupleness.' They stop growing as individuals and the relationship stagnates. They may stop making healthy individual or couple changes and instead, settle for lukewarm compromises. To keep their relationship healthy, couples must take care to maintain personal and emotional boundaries and guard against complacency.

For **emotionally-expressive** couples, life is never dull. Of all the couple styles, this one yields the richest emotional experience and the least security. Such couples are highly emotionally engaged and share the gamut of feelings, from joy to anger. While this is a strength, its benefits are somewhat neutralized by the fact that empathetic listening and moral support are not highly valued. Partner A's expressions of feelings, perceptions and opinions are intertwined with efforts to persuade B to see things his/her way and act the way (s)he wants B to act. Healthy emotionally expressive couples do not sucker-punch each other in an argument or threaten retaliation if wronged. There is little complacency in these relationships. Such partners view individual and couple changes as positive; routinization of the relationship as detrimental. The biggest trap an emotionally expressive couple can fall into that of conflict becoming a juggernaut; steamrolling over the couple and crushing the bond between them. Arguments can become power struggles resulting in unilateral, self-defeating decisions. If the relationship is to remain healthy, the couple must take care in the event of an argument not to wield such weapons as humiliation, threats or betrayal.

Relationship Maintenance Strategies

Q: How do you make a marriage work?

- A: Tell your wife she looks pretty, even if she looks like a truck. (Ricky, age 10)

Q: What do you think your mom and dad have in common?

- A: Both don't want any more kids. (Lori, age 8)

People who are committed to keeping their relationship healthy and viable over time think and (inter)act differently than do less committed couples (Reesing and Cate, 2004). They speak in terms of *we, us* and *ours* instead of *I, me* and *mine* (Agnew et. al., 1998). They ignore others who try to lure them into an 'extracurricular' relationship. Each works to achieve a balance between having it his/her own way and allowing the partner's preferences to prevail, whether in the arena of recreational activities (e.g. which restaurant to go to) or household projects (e.g. what color to paint the living room). They encourage and support each other's pursuit of personal and professional goals. They tolerate each other's occasional bad moods and thoughtless acts. Each responds constructively to any criticisms or provocations from the other, rather than 'biting' back. They forgive each other's *minor* wrongdoings and betrayals.

Via his study of married couples, Olson (2000) found qualitative differences between happy and unhappy couples in five important areas: communication, flexibility, emotional closeness, personality compatibility and constructive handling of conflicts. He noted five additional areas that impact relationship happiness: the couple's sexual relationship, choice of leisure activities, influence of family and friends, ability to manage finances and sharing of religious beliefs.

Based on his own research, Gottman (1994) found the best predictors of relationship unhappiness, breakups and divorce were what he called *"The Four Horsemen of the Apocalypse:"*

- Criticism–attaching the partner's personality or character rather than identifying specific behaviors that are of concern
- Contempt–insults, mockery, hostile humor
- Defensiveness–making excuses or counter-attacking
- Stonewalling–listener withdrawal; clamming up, "the silent treatment"

Additional studies (Gottman, Coan, Carrere and Swanson, 1998) indicate that **belligerence**–the in-your-face sort of taunts designed to escalate rather than resolve a conflict, e.g. "Whaddya gonna do about it? Just try and stop me!"–have an equally corrosive effect on relationships.

It appears, in short, that couples who are open and constructive with each other; who share tasks and recreational activities, who have friends in common, who take the time to assure each other of their love and commitment and who are typically in good spirits, are likely to be happy together over time (Canary et. al., 2002; Dainton, 2000).

REFERENCES

ABC News 20/20 (August 30, 1998). *Love, lust and marriage: Why we stay and why we stray.* Host: John Stossel.

Agnew, C.R., Van Lange, P.A.M., Rusbult, C.E. & Langston, C.A. (1998). Cognitive interdependence: commitment and the mental representation of close relationships. *Journal of Personality and Social Psychology, 74,* 939–954.

Argyle, M., & Henderson, M. (1985). The anatomy of friendships. London: Penguin.

Baxter, L.A. (1986) Gender differences in the heterosexual relationship rules embedded in break-up accounts. *Journal of Social and Personal Relationships, 3,* 289–306.

Berscheid, E., & Walster, E., (1978). *Interpersonal Attraction.* Reading, MA: Addison-Wesley.

Burleson, B.R. (1994). Comforting messages: Features, functions, and outcomes. In J. A. Daly & J. M. Wiemann (Eds.), *Strategic interpersonal communication* (pp. 135–162). Hillsdale, NJ: Erlbaum.

Canary, D.J., Stafford, L. & Semic, B.A. (2002). A panel study of the associations between maintenance strategies and relational characteristics. *Journal of Marriage and the Family, 64,* 395–406.

Dainton, M. (2000). Maintenance behaviors, expectations for maintenance and satisfaction: Linking comparison levels to relational maintenance strategies. *Journal of Social and Personal Relationships, 17,* 827–842.

Fehr, B. (1996). *Friendship processes.* Thousand Oaks, CA: Sage.

Gottman, J.M. (1994). What predicts divorce? The relationship between marital *processes and marital outcomes.* Hillsdale, NJ: Erlbaum.

Gottman, J.M., Coan, J., Carrère, S. & Swanson, C. (1998). Predicting marital happiness and stability from newlywed interactions. *Journal of Marriage and the* Family, 60, 5–22.

Harris, J. (2003). *I kissed dating goodbye.* Sisters, OR: Multnomah.

Hays, R.B. (1985). A longitudinal study of friendship development. *Journal of Personal and Social Psychology, 48,* 909–924.

Landers, A. (1982). *Love or sex . . . and how to tell the difference.* Chicago: Field Enterprises.

McCarthy, B., & McCarthy, E. (2004). *Getting it right the first time: creating a healthy Marriage* (pp. 25–46). Florence, KY: Routledge.

Miller, R.S., Perlman, D. & Brehm., S.S.(2007). *Intimate Relationships.* New York: McGraw-Hill.

National Public Radio (June 10, 2004). *Talk of the Nation* broadcast. Host: Neal Conan.

Olson, D. (2000). *Empowering Couples: Building on Your Strengths.* Minneapolis: Life Innovations.

Reesing, A.L. & Cate, R.M. (July 2004). *Relationship commitment and its association* with relationship maintenance: An application of the commitment framework. Paper presented at a meeting of the International Association for Relationship Research, Madison, WI.

Sternberg, R.J. (1987). *The triangle of love: Intimacy, passion, commitment.* New York: Basic Books.

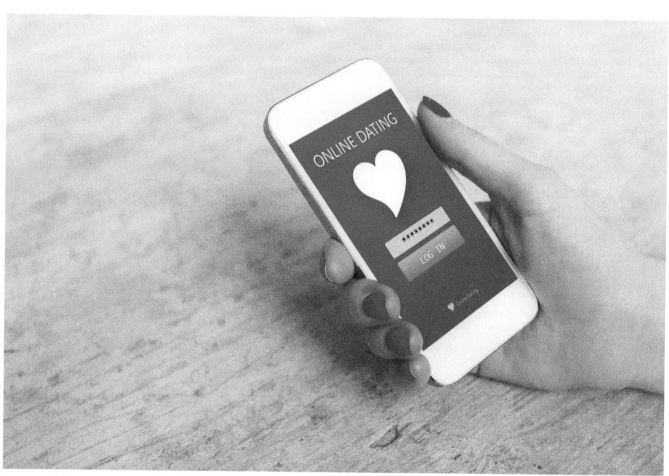

Shutterstock/Kaspars Grinvalds

12

NEW TECHNOLOGIES AND OUR FEELINGS
Romance on the Internet

CHRISTINE ROSEN

When Samuel F. B. Morse sent his first long-distance telegraph message in 1844, he chose words that emphasized both the awe and apprehension he felt about his new device. "What hath God wrought?" read the paper tape message of dots and dashes sent from the U.S. Capitol building to Morse's associates in Baltimore. Morse proved prescient about the potential scope and significance of his technology. In less than a decade, telegraph wires spread throughout all but one state east of the Mississippi River; by 1861, they spanned the continent; and by 1866, a transatlantic telegraph cable connected the United States to Europe.

The telegraph, and later, the telephone, forever changed the way we communicate. But the triumph wrought by these technologies was not merely practical. Subtly and not so subtly, these technologies also altered the range of ways we reveal ourselves. Writing in 1884, James Russell Lowell wondered a bit nervously about the long-term consequences of the "trooping of emotion" that the electric telegraph, with its fragmented messages, encouraged. Lowell and others feared that the sophisticated new media we were devising might alter not just how we communicate, but how we feel.

Rapid improvement in communication technologies and the expansion of their practical uses continue unabated. Today, of course, we are no longer tethered to telegraph or telephone wires for conversation. Cell phones, e-mail, Internet chatrooms, two-way digital cameras — we can talk to anyone, anywhere, including those we do not know and never see. The ethical challenges raised by these new communication technologies are legion, and not new. Within a decade of the invention of the telephone, for example, we had designed a way to wiretap and listen in on the private conversations flourishing there. And with the Internet, we can create new or false identities for ourselves, mixing real life and personal fantasy in unpredictable ways. The "confidence man" of the nineteenth century, with his dandified ruses, is replaced by the well-chosen screen name and false autobiography of the unscrupulous Internet dater. Modern philosophers of technology have studied the ethical quandaries posed by communication technologies — questioning whether our view of new technologies as simply means to generally positive ends is naïve, and encouraging us to consider whether our many devices have effected subtle transformations on our natures.

But too little consideration has been given to the question of how our use of these technologies influences our emotions. Do certain methods of communication flatten emotional appeals, promote immediacy rather than thoughtful reflection, and encourage accessibility and transparency at the expense of necessary boundaries? Do our technologies change the way we feel, act, and think?

Love and E-Mail

There is perhaps no realm in which this question has more salience than that of romantic love. How do our ubiquitous technologies — cell phones, e-mail, the Internet — impact our ability to find and experience love? Our technical devices are of such extraordinary practical use that we forget they are also increasingly the primary medium for our emotional expression. The technologies we use on a daily basis do not merely change the ways, logistically, we pursue love; they are in some cases transforming the way we think and feel about what, exactly, it is we should be pursuing. They change not simply how we find our beloved, but the kind of beloved we hope to find. In a world where men and women still claim to want to find that one special person — a "soul mate" — to spend their life with, what role can and should we afford technology and, more broadly, science, in their efforts?

Love after Courtship

The pursuit of love in its modern, technological guise has its roots in the decline of courtship and is indelibly marked by that loss. Courtship as it once existed — a practice that assumed adherence to certain social conventions, and recognition of the differences, physical and emotional, between men and women — has had its share of pleased obituarists. The most vigorous have been feminists, the more radical of whom appear to take special delight in quelling notions of romantic love. Recall Andrea Dworkin's infamous equation of marriage and rape, or Germaine Greer's terrifying rant in *The Female Eunuch:* "Love, love, love — all the wretched cant of it, masking egotism, lust, masochism, fantasy under a mythology of sentimental postures, a welter of self-induced miseries and joys, blinding and masking the essential personalities in the frozen gestures of courtship, in the kissing and the dating and the desire, the compliments and the quarrels which vivify its barrenness." Much of this work is merely an unpersuasive attempt to swaddle basic human bitterness in the language of female empowerment. But such sentiments have had their effect on our culture's understanding of courtship.

More thoughtful chroniclers of the institution's demise have noted the cultural and technological forces that challenged courtship in the late nineteenth and early twentieth century, eroding the power of human chaperones, once its most effective guardians. As Leon Kass persuasively argued in an essay in *The Public Interest,* the obstacles to courtship "spring from the very heart of liberal democratic society and of modernity altogether." The automobile did more for unsupervised sexual exploration than many technologies in use today, for example, and by twentieth century's end, the ease and availability of effective contraceptive devices, especially the birth control pill, had freed men and women to pursue sexual experience without the risk of pregnancy. With technical advances came a shift in social mores. As historian Jacques Barzun has noted, strict manners gave way to informality, "for etiquette is a barrier, the casual style an invitation."

Whether one laments or praises courtship's decline, it is clear that we have yet to locate a successful replacement for it — evidently it is not as simple as hustling the aging coquette out the door to make way for the vigorous debutante. On the contrary, our current courting practices — if they can be called that — yield an increasing number of those aging coquettes, as well as scores of unsettled bachelors. On college campuses, young men and women have long since ceased formally dating and instead participate in a "hooking up" culture that favors the sexually promiscuous and emotionally disinterested while punishing those intent on commitment. Adults hardly fare better: as the author of a report released in January by the Chicago Health and Social Life Survey told CNN, "on average, half your life is going to be in this single and dating state, and this is a big change from the 1950s." Many men and women now spend the decades of their twenties and thirties sampling each other's sexual wares and engaging in fits of serial out-of-wedlock domesticity, never finding a marriageable partner.

In the 1990s, books such as *The Rules,* which outlined a rigorous and often self-abnegating plan for modern dating, and observers such as Wendy Shalit, who called for greater modesty and the withholding of sexual favors by women, represented a well-intentioned, if doomed, attempt to revive the old courting boundaries. Cultural observers today, however, claim we are in the midst of a new social revolution that requires looking to the future for solutions, not the past. "We're in a period of dramatic change in our mating practices," Barbara Dafoe Whitehead told a reporter for *U.S. News & World Report* recently. Whitehead, co-director of the National Marriage Project at Rutgers University, is the author of *Why There are No Good Men Left,* one in a booming mini-genre of books that offer road maps for the revolution. Whitehead views technology as one of our best solutions — Isolde can now find her Tristan on the Internet (though presumably with a less tragic finale). "The traditional mating system where people met someone in their neighborhood or college is pretty much dead," Whitehead told CBS recently. "What we have is a huge population of working singles who have limited opportunities to go through some elaborate courtship."

Although Whitehead is correct in her diagnosis of the problem, neither she nor the mavens of modesty offer a satisfactory answer to this new challenge. A return to the old rules and rituals of courtship — however appealing in theory — is neither practical nor desirable for the majority of men and women. But the uncritical embrace of technological solutions to our romantic malaise — such as Internet dating — is not a long-term solution either. What we need to do is create new boundaries, devise better guideposts, and enforce new mores for our technological age. First, however, we must understand the peculiar challenges to romantic success posed by our technologies.

Full Disclosure

Although not the root cause of our romantic malaise, our communication technologies are at least partly culpable, for they encourage the erosion of the boundaries that are necessary for the growth of successful relationships. Our technologies enable and often promote two detrimental forces in modern relationships: the demand for total transparency and a bias toward the over-sharing of personal information.

To Google or Not to Google

With the breakdown of the old hierarchies and boundaries that characterized courtship, there are far fewer opportunities to glean information about the vast world of strangers we encounter daily. We can little rely on town gossips or networks of extended kin for background knowledge; there are far fewer geographic boundaries marking people from "the good part of town"; no longer can we read sartorial signals, such as a well-cut suit or an expensive shoe, to place people as in earlier ages. This is all, for the most part, a good thing. But how, then, do people find out about each other? Few self-possessed people with an Internet connection could resist answering that question with one word: Google. "To google" — now an acceptable if ill-begotten verb — is the practice of typing a person's name into an Internet search engine to find out what the world knows and says about him or her. As one writer confessed in the *New York Observer,* after meeting an attractive man at a midtown bar: "Like many of my twenty-something peers in New York's dating jungle, I have begun to use Google.com, as well as other online search engines, to perform secret background checks on potential mates. It's not perfect, but it's a discreet way of obtaining important, useless and sometimes bizarre information about people in Manhattan — and it's proven to be as reliable as the scurrilous gossip you get from friends."

That is — not reliable at all. What Google and other Internet search engines provide is a quick glimpse — a best and worst list — of a person, not a fully drawn portrait. In fact, the transparency promised by technologies such as Internet search engines is a convenient substitute for something we used to assume would develop over time, but which fewer people today seem willing to cultivate patiently: trust. As the single Manhattanite writing in the *Observer* noted, "You never know. He seemed nice that night, but he could be anyone from a rapist or murderer to a brilliant author or championship swimmer."

In sum, transparency does not guarantee trust. It can, in fact, prove effective at eroding it — especially when the expectation of transparency and the available technological tools nudge the suspicious to engage in more invasive forms of investigation or surveillance. One woman I interviewed, who asked that her name not be revealed, was suspicious that her live-in boyfriend of two years was unfaithful when her own frequent business trips took her away from home. Unwilling to confront him directly with her doubts, she turned to a technological solution. Unbeknownst to him, she installed a popular brand of "spyware" on his computer, which recorded every keystroke he made and took snapshots of his screen every three minutes — information that the program then e-mailed to her for inspection. "My suspicions were founded," she said, although the revelation was hardly good news. "He was spending hours online looking at porn, and going to 'hook-up' chatrooms seeking sex with strangers. I even tracked his ATM withdrawals to locations near his scheduled meetings with other women."

She ended the relationship, but remains unrepentant about deploying surveillance technology against her mate. Considering the amount of information she could find out about her partner by merely surfing the Internet, she rationalized her use of spyware as just one more tool — if a slightly more invasive one — at the disposal of those seeking information about another person. As our technologies give us ever-greater power to uncover more about each other, demand for transparency rises, and our expectations of privacy decline.

The other destructive tendency our technologies encourage is over-sharing — that is, revealing too much, too quickly, in the hope of connecting to another person. The opportunities for instant communication are so ubiquitous — e-mail, instant messaging, chatrooms, cell phones, Palm Pilots, BlackBerrys, and the like — that the notion of making ourselves unavailable to anyone is unheard of, and constant access a near-requirement. As a result, the multitude of outlets for expressing ourselves has allowed the level of idle chatter to reach a depressing din. The inevitable result is a repeal of the reticence necessary for fostering successful relationships in the long term. Information about another person is best revealed a bit at a time, in a give-and-take exchange, not in a rush of overexposed feeling.

The Bachelor

Perhaps the best example of this tendency is reality TV and its spawn. Programs like *The Bachelor* and *The Bachelorette,* as well as pseudo-documentary shows such as *A Dating Story* (and *A Wedding Story* and *A Baby Story*) on The Learning Channel, transform the longings of the human heart into top Nielsen ratings by encouraging the lovelorn to discuss in depth and at length every feeling they have, every moment they have it, as the cameras roll. Romances begin, blossom, and occasionally end in the space of half an hour, and audiences — privy to even the most excruciatingly staged expressions of love and devotion — nevertheless gain the illusion of having seen "real" examples of dating, wedding, or marriage.

On the Internet, dating blogs offer a similar sophomoric voyeurism. One dating blogger, who calls himself Quigley, keeps a dreary tally of his many unsuccessful attempts to meet women, peppering his diary with adolescent observations about women he sees on television. Another dating blogger, who describes herself as an "attractive 35-year old," writes "A Day in the Life of Jane," a dating diary about her online dating travails. Reflecting on one of her early experiences, she writes: "But what did I learn from Owen? That online dating isn't so different from regular dating. It has its pros and cons: Pros – you learn a lot more about a person much more quickly, that a person isn't always what they seem or what you believe them to be, that you have to be really honest with yourself and the person you are communicating with; Cons – uh, same as the pros!"

BadXPartners.com

Successful relationships are not immune to the over-sharing impulse, either; a plethora of wedding websites such as Sharethe-Moments.com and TheKnot.com offer up the intimate details of couples' wedding planning and ceremonies – right down to the brand of tie worn by the groom and the "intimate" vows exchanged by the couple. And, if things go awry, there are an increasing number of revenge websites such as BadXPartners.com, which offers people who've been dumped an opportunity for petty revenge. "Create a comical case file of your BadXPartners for the whole world to see!" the website urges. Like the impulse to Google, the site plays on people's fears of being misled, encouraging people to search the database for stories of bad exes: "Just met someone new? Think they are just the one for you? Well remember, they are probably someone else's X. . . . Find out about Bill from Birmingham's strange habits or Tracy from Texas' suspect hygiene. Better safe than sorry!"

Like the steady work of the wrecking ball, our culture's nearly-compulsive demand for personal revelation, emotional exposure, and sharing of feelings threatens the fragile edifice of newly-forming relationships. Transparency and complete access are exactly what you want to avoid in the early stages of romance. Successful courtship – even successful flirtation – require the gradual peeling away of layers, some deliberately constructed, others part of a person's character and personality, that make us mysteries to each other.

Among Pascal's minor works is an essay, "Discourse on the Passion of Love," in which he argues for the keen "pleasure of loving without daring to tell it." "In love," Pascal writes, "silence is of more avail than speech . . . there is an eloquence in silence that penetrates more deeply than language can." Pascal imagined his lovers in each other's physical presence, watchful of unspoken physical gestures, but not speaking. Only gradually would they reveal themselves. Today such a tableau seems as arcane as Kabuki theater; modern couples exchange the most intimate details of their lives on a first date and then return home to blog about it.

"It's difficult," said one woman I talked to who has tried – and ultimately soured on – Internet dating. "You're expected to be both informal and funny in your e-mails, and reveal your likes and dislikes, but you don't want to reveal so much that you appear desperate, or so little so that you seem distant." We can, of course, use these technologies appropriately and effectively in the service of advancing a relationship, but to do so both people must understand the potential dangers. One man I interviewed described a relationship that began promisingly but quickly took a technological turn for the worse. After a few successful dates, he encouraged the woman he was seeing, who lived in another city, to keep in touch. Impervious to notions of technological etiquette, however, she took this to mean the floodgates were officially open. She began telephoning him at all hours, sending overlywrought e-mails and inundating him with lengthy, faxed letters – all of which had the effect not of bringing them closer together, which was clearly her hope, but of sending him scurrying away as fast as he could. Later, however, he became involved in a relationship in which e-mail in particular helped facilitate the courtship, and where technology – bounded by a respect on the part of both people for its excesses – helped rather than harmed the process of learning about another person. Technology itself is not to blame; it is our ignorance of its potential dangers and our unwillingness to exercise self-restraint in its use that makes mischief.

The Modern-Day Matchmaker

Internet dating offers an interesting case study of these technological risks, for it encourages both transparency and over-sharing, as well as another danger: it insists that we reduce and market ourselves as the disembodied sum of our parts. The woman or man you might have met on the subway platform or in a coffee shop – within a richer context that includes immediate impressions based on the other person's physical gestures, attire, tone of voice, and overall demeanor – is instead electronically embalmed for your efficient perusal online.

And it is a booming business. Approximately forty percent of American adults are single, and half of that population claims to have visited an online dating site. Revenue for online dating services exceeded $302 million in 2002. There is, not surprisingly, something for the profusion of tastes: behemoth sites such as Match.com, Flirt.com, Hypermatch.com, and Matchmaker.com traffic in thousands of profiles. Niche sites such as Dateable.org for people with disabilities, as well as sites devoted to finding true love for foot fetishists, animal lovers, and the obese, cater to smaller markets. Single people with religious preferences can visit Jdate.com (for Jewish dates), CatholicSingles.com, and even HappyBuddhist.com to find similarly-minded spiritual singles. As with any product, new features are added constantly to maintain consumer interest; even the more jaded seekers of love might quail at Match.com's recent addition to its menu of online options: a form of "speed dating" that offers a certain brutal efficiency as a lure for the time-challenged modern singleton.

A Case Study

One woman I interviewed, an attractive, successful consultant, tried online dating because her hectic work schedule left her little time to meet new people. She went to Match.com, entered her zip code, and began perusing profiles. She quickly decided to post her own. "When you first put your profile on Match.com," she said, "it's like walking into a kennel with a pork chop around your neck. You're bombarded with e-mails from men." She received well over one hundred solicitations. She responded to a few with a "wink," an electronic gesture that allows another person to know you've seen their profile and are interested — but not interested enough to commit to sending an e-mail message. More alluring profiles garnered an e-mail introduction.

After meeting several different men for coffee, she settled on one in particular and they dated for several months. The vagaries of online dating, however, quickly present new challenges to relationship etiquette. In her case, after several months of successful dating, she and her boyfriend agreed to take their Match.com profiles down from the site. Since they were no longer "single and looking," but single and dating, this seemed to make sense — at least to her. Checking Match.com a week later, however, she found her boyfriend's profile still up and actively advertising himself as available. They are still together, although she confesses to a new wariness about his willingness to commit.

The rapid growth of Internet dating has led to the erosion of the stigma that used to be attached to having "met someone on the Internet" (although none of the people I interviewed for this article would allow their names to be used). And Internet dating itself is becoming increasingly professionalized — with consultants, how-to books, and "expert" analysis crowding out the earlier generation of websites. This February, a "commonsense guide to successful Internet dating" entitled *I Can't Believe I'm Buying This Book* hit bookstores. *Publishers Weekly* describes the author, an "Internet dating consultant," as "a self-proclaimed online serial dater" who "admits he's never sustained a relationship for more than seven months," yet nevertheless "entertainingly reviews how to present one's self on the Web."

Designing the "dating software" that facilitates online romance is a science all its own. *U.S. News & World Report* recently described the efforts of Michael Georgeff, who once designed software to aid the space shuttle program, to devise similar algorithms to assess and predict people's preferences for each other. "Say you score a 3 on the introvert scale, and a 6 on touchy-feely," he told a reporter. "Will you tend to like somebody who's practical?" His weAttract.com software purports to provide the answer. On the company's Web site, amid close-ups of the faces of a strangely androgynous, snuggling couple, weAttract — whose software is used by Match.com — encourages visitors to "Find someone who considers your quirks adorable." Fair enough. But the motto of weAttract — "Discover your instinctual preferences" — is itself a contradiction. If preferences are instinctual, why do you need the aid of experts like weAttract to discover them?

We need them because we have come to mistrust our own sensibilities. What is emerging on the Internet is a glorification of scientific and technological solutions to the challenge of finding love. The expectation of romantic happiness is so great that extraordinary, scientific means for achieving it are required — or so these companies would have you believe. For example, Emode, whose pop-up ads are now so common that they are the Internet equivalent of a swarm of pesky gnats, promotes "Tickle Matchmaking," a service promising "accurate, Ph.D. certified compatibility scores with every member!"

EHarmony.com

The apotheosis of this way of thinking is a site called eHarmony.com, whose motto, "Fall in love for the right reasons," soothes prospective swains with the comforting rhetoric of professional science. "Who knew science and love were so compatible?" asks the site, which is rife with the language of the laboratory: "scientifically-proven set of compatibility principles," "based on 35 years of empirical and clinical research," "patent-pending matching technology," "exhaustively researched" methods, and "the most powerful system available." As the founder of eHarmony told *U.S. News & World Report* recently, we are all too eager — desperate, even — to hustle down the aisle. "In this culture," he said, "if we like the person's looks, if they have an ability to chatter at a cocktail party, and a little bit of status, we're halfway to marriage. We're such suckers." EHarmony's answer to such unscientific mating practices is a trademarked "Compatibility Matching System" that promises to "connect you with singles who are compatible with you in 29 of the most important areas of life." As the literature constantly reminds the dreamy romantics among us, "Surprisingly, a good match is more science than art."

EHarmony's insistence that the search for true love is no realm for amateurs is, of course, absurdly self-justifying. "You should realize," their Web site admonishes, after outlining the "29 dimensions" of personality their compatibility software examines, "that it is still next to impossible to correctly evaluate them on your own with each person you think may be right for you." Instead you must pay eHarmony to do it for you. As you read the "scientific" proof, the reassuring sales pitch washes over you: "Let eHarmony make sure that the next time you fall in love, it's with the right person."

In other words, don't trust your instincts, trust science. With a tasteful touch of contempt, eHarmony notes that its purpose is not merely dating, as it is for megasites such as Match.com. "Our goal is to help you find your soul mate." Four pages of testimonials on the website encourage the surrender to eHarmony's expertise, with promises of imminent collision with "your" soul mate: "From the minute we began e-mailing and talking on the phone, we knew we had found our soul mate," say Lisa and Darryl from Dover, Pennsylvania. "It took some time," confessed Annie of Kansas City, Missouri, "but once I met John, I knew that they had made good on their promise to help me find my soul mate."

Some observers see in these new "scientific" mating rituals a return to an earlier time of courtship and chaperoned dating. *Newsweek* eagerly described eHarmony as a form of "arranged marriage for the digital age, without the all-powerful parents," and Barbara Dafoe Whitehead argues that the activities of the Internet love seeker "reflect a desire for more structured dating." Promoters of these services see them as an improvement on the mere cruising of glossy photos encouraged by most dating sites, or the unrealistic expectations of "finding true love" promoted by popular culture. Rather, they say, they are like the chaperones of courtship past — vetting appropriate candidates and matching them to your specifications.

Not Real Matchmakers

As appealing as this might sound, it is unrealistic. Since these sites rely on technological solutions and mathematical algorithms, they are a far cry from the broader and richer knowledge of the old-fashioned matchmaker. A personality quiz cannot possibly reveal the full range of a person's quirks or liabilities. More importantly, the role of the old-fashioned matchmaker was a social one (and still is in certain communities). The matchmaker was embedded within a community that observed certain rituals and whose members shared certain assumptions. But technological matchmaking allows courtship to be conducted entirely in private, devoid of the social norms (and often the physical signals) of romantic success and failure.

Finally, most Internet dating enthusiasts do not contend with a far more alarming challenge: the impact such services have on our idea of what, exactly, it is we should be seeking in another person. Younger men and women, weaned on the Internet and e-mail, are beginning to express a preference for potential dates to break down their vital stats for pre-date perusal, like an Internet dating advertisement. One 25-year old man, a regular on Match.com, confessed to *U.S. News & World Report* that he wished he could have a digital dossier for all of his potential dates: "It's, 'OK, here's where I'm from, here's what I do, here's what I'm looking for. How about you?'" One woman I spoke to, who has been Internet dating for several years, matter-of-factly noted that even a perfunctory glance at a potential date's résumé saves valuable time and energy. "Why trust a glance exchanged across a crowded bar when you can read a person's biography in miniature before deciding to strike up a conversation?" she said. This intolerance for gradual revelation increases the pace of modern courtship and erodes our patience for many things (not the least of which is commencement of sexual relations). The challenge remains the same — to find another person to share your life with — but we have allowed the technologies at our disposal to alter dramatically, even unrecognizably, the way we go about achieving it.

The Science of Feeling

This impulse is part of a much broader phenomenon — the encroachment of science and technology into areas once thought the province of the uniquely intuitive and even the ineffable. Today we program computers to trounce human chess champions, produce poetry, or analyze works of art, watching eagerly as they break things down to a tedious catalog of techniques: the bishop advances, the meter scans, the paintbrush strokes across the canvas. But by enlisting machines to do what once was the creative province of human beings alone, we deliberately narrow our conceptions of genius, creativity, and art. The *New York Times* recently featured the work of Franco Moretti, a comparative literature professor at Stanford, who promotes "a more rational literary history" that jettisons the old-fashioned reading of texts in favor of statistical models of literary output. His dream, he told reporter Emily Eakin, "is of a literary class that would look more like a lab than a Platonic academy."

Yet this "scientific" approach to artistic work yields chillingly antiseptic results: "Tennyson's mind is to be treated like his intestines after a barium meal," historian Jacques Barzun noted with some exasperation of the trend's earlier incarnations. Critic Lionel Trilling parodied the tendency in 1950 in his book, *The Liberal Imagination*. By this way of thinking, Trilling said, the story of Romeo and Juliet is no longer the tragic tale of a young man and woman falling in love, but becomes instead a chronicle of how, "their libidinal impulses being reciprocal, they activated their individual erotic drives and integrated them within the same frame of reference."

What Barzun and Trilling were expressing was a distaste for viewing art as merely an abstraction of measurable, improvable impulses. The same is true for love. We can study the physiological functions of the human heart with echocardiograms, stress tests, blood pressure readings, and the like. We can examine, analyze, and investigate ad nauseum the physical act of sex. But we cannot so easily measure the desires of the heart. How do you prove that love exists? How do we know that love is "real"? What makes the love of two lovers last?

There is a danger in relying wholly or even largely on science and technology to answer these questions, for it risks eroding our appreciation of the ineffable things — intuition and physical attraction, passion and sensibility — by reducing these feelings to scientifically explained physiological facts. Today we catalog the influence of hormones, pheromones, dopamine, and serotonin in human attraction, and map our own brains to discover which synapses trigger laughter, lying, or orgasm. Evolutionary psychology explains our desire for symmetrical faces and fertile-looking forms, even as it has little to tell us about the extremes to which we are taking its directives with plastic surgery. Scientific study of our communication patterns and techniques explains why it is we talk the way we do. Even the activities of the bedroom are thoroughly analyzed and professionalized, as women today take instruction from a class of professionals whose arts used to be less esteemed. Prostitutes now run sex seminars, for example, and a recent episode of Oprah featured exotic pole dancers who teach suburban housewives how to titillate their husbands by turning the basement rec room into a simulacrum of a Vegas showgirl venue.

Science continues to turn sex (and, by association, love and romance) into something quantifiable and open to manipulation and solution. Science and technology offer us pharmaceuticals to enhance libido and erectile function, and popular culture responds by rigorously ranking and discussing all matters sexual — from the disturbingly frank talk of female characters on Sex and the City to the proliferation of "blind date" shows which subject hapless love-seekers to the withering gaze of a sarcastic host and his viewing audience. "What a loser!" cackled the host of the reality television program Blind Date, after one ignominious bachelor botched his chance for a good night kiss. "The march of science," Barzun wrote, "produces the feeling that nobody in the past has ever done things right. Whether it's teaching or copulation, it has 'problems' that 'research' should solve by telling us just how, the best way."

Test-Driving Your Soul Mate

Why is the steady march of science and technology in these areas a problem? Shouldn't we be proud of our expanding knowledge and the tools that knowledge gives us? Not necessarily. Writing recently in the journal *Techné*, Hector Jose Huyke noted the broader dangers posed by the proliferation of our technologies, particularly the tendency to "devalue the near." "When a technology is introduced it, presumably, simply adds options to already existing options," he writes. But this is not how technology's influence plays out in practice. In fact, as Huyke argues, "as what is difficult to obtain becomes repeatedly and easily accessible, other practices and experiences are left out — they do not remain unchanged." The man who sends an e-mail to his brother is not merely choosing to write an e-mail and thus adding to his range of communication options; he is choosing not to make a phone call or write a letter. A woman who e-mails a stranger on the Internet is choosing not to go to a local art exhibit and perhaps meet someone in person. "Communications technologies indeed multiply options," says Huyke. "An increase in options, however, does not imply or even serve an advance in communications." Technologies, in other words, often make possible "what would otherwise be difficult to obtain." But they do so by eliminating other paths.

Personal Ads

Love and genuine commitment have always been difficult to attain, and they are perhaps more so today since it is the individual bonds of affection — not family alliance, property transfer, social class, or religious orthodoxy — that form the cornerstone of most modern marriages. Yet there remains a certain grim efficiency to the vast realm of love technologies at our disposal. After a while, perusing Internet personal ads is like being besieged by an aggressive real estate agent hoping to unload that tired brick colonial. Each person points out his or her supposedly unique features with the same banal descriptions ("adventurous," "sexy," "trustworthy") never conveying a genuine sense of the whole. Machine metaphors, tellingly, crop up often, with women and men willingly categorizing themselves as "high maintenance" or "low maintenance," much as one might describe a car or small kitchen appliance. As an executive of one online dating service told a reporter recently, "If you want to buy a car, you get a lot of information before you even test-drive. There hasn't been a way to do that with relationships."

But we have been "test driving" something: a new, technological method of courtship. And although it is too soon to deliver a final verdict, it is clear that it is a method prone to serious problems. The efficiency of our new techniques and their tendency to focus on people as products leaves us at risk of understanding ourselves this way, too — like products with certain malfunctioning parts and particular assets. But products must be constantly improved upon and marketed. In the pursuit of love, and in a world where multiple partners are sampled before one is selected, this fuels a hectic culture of self-improvement — honing the witty summary of one's most desirable traits for placement in personal advertisements is only the beginning. Today, men and women convene focus groups of former lovers to gain critical insights into their behavior so as to avoid future failure; and the perfection of appearance through surgical and non-surgical means occupies an increasing amount of people's time and energy.

Our new technological methods of courtship also elevate efficient communication over personal communication. Ironically, the Internet, which offers many opportunities to meet and communicate with new people, robs us of the ability to deploy one of our greatest charms — nonverbal communication. The emoticon is a weak substitute for a coy gesture or a lusty wink. More fundamentally, our technologies encourage a misunderstanding of what courtship should be. Real courtship is about persuasion, not marketing, and the techniques of the laboratory cannot help us translate the motivations of the heart.

The response is not to retreat into Luddism, of course. In a world where technology allows us to meet, date, marry, and even divorce online, there is no returning to the innocence of an earlier time. What we need is a better understanding of the risks of these new technologies and a willingness to exercise restraint in using them. For better or worse, we are now a society of sexually liberated individuals seeking "soul mates" — yet the privacy, gradualism, and boundaries that are necessary for separating the romantic wheat from the chaff still elude us.

Alchemy

Perhaps, in our technologically saturated age, we would do better to rediscover an earlier science: alchemy. Not alchemy in its original meaning — a branch of speculative philosophy whose devotees attempted to create gold from base metals and hence cure disease and prolong life — but alchemy in its secondary definition: "a power or process of transforming something common into something precious." From our daily, common interactions with other people might spring something precious — but only if we have the patience to let it flourish. Technology and science often conspire against such patience. Goethe wrote, "We should do our utmost to encourage the Beautiful, for the Useful encourages itself." There is an eminent usefulness to many of our technologies — e-mail and cell phones allow us to span great distances to communicate with family, friends, and lovers, and the Internet connects us to worlds unknown. But they are less successful at encouraging the flourishing of the lasting and beautiful. Like the Beautiful, love occurs in unexpected places, often not where it is being sought. It can flourish only if we accept that our technologies and our science can never fully explain it.

Christine Rosen is a senior editor of *The New Atlantis* and resident fellow at the Ethics and Public Policy Center. Her book *Preaching Eugenics: Religious Leaders and the American Eugenics Movement* was just published by Oxford University Press.
"Romance in the Information Age," *The New Atlantis,* Winter 2004, pp. 3-16. Copyright © 2004 by Ethics & Public Policy Center. Reprinted by permission.

Design Pics/Darren Greenwood

13

THIS THING CALLED LOVE

LAUREN SLATER

My husband and I got married at eight in the morning. It was winter, freezing, the trees encased in ice and a few lone blackbirds balancing on telephone wires. We were in our early 30s, considered ourselves hip and cynical, the types who decried the institution of marriage even as we sought its status. During our wedding brunch we put out a big suggestion box and asked people to slip us advice on how to avoid divorce; we thought it was a funny, clear-eyed, grounded sort of thing to do, although the suggestions were mostly foolish: Screw the toothpaste cap on tight. After the guests left, the house got quiet. There were flowers everywhere: puckered red roses and fragile ferns. "What can we do that's really romantic?" I asked my newly wed one. Benjamin suggested we take a bath. I didn't want a bath. He suggested a lunch of chilled white wine and salmon. I was sick of salmon.

What can we do that's really romantic? The wedding was over, the silence seemed suffocating, and I felt the familiar disappointment after a longed-for event has come and gone. We were married. Hip, hip, hooray. I decided to take a walk. I went into the center of town, pressed my nose against a bakery window, watched the man with flour on his hands, the dough as soft as skin, pushed and pulled and shaped at last into stars. I milled about in an antique store. At last I came to our town's tattoo parlor. Now I am not a tattoo type person, but for some reason, on that cold silent Sunday, I decided to walk in. "Can I help you?" a woman asked.

"Is there a kind of tattoo I can get that won't be permanent?" I asked.

"Henna tattoos," she said.

She explained that they lasted for six weeks, were used at Indian weddings, were stark and beautiful and all brown. She showed me pictures of Indian women with jewels in their noses, their arms scrolled and laced with the henna markings. Indeed they were beautiful, sharing none of the gaudy comic strip quality of the tattoos we see in the United States. These henna tattoos spoke of intricacy, of the webwork between two people, of ties that bind and how difficult it is to find their beginnings and their elms. And because I had just gotten married, and because I was feeling a post wedding letdown, and because I wanted something really romantic to sail me through the night, I decided to get one.

"Where?" she asked.

"Here," I said. I laid my hands over my breasts and belly.

She raised her eyebrows. "Sure," she said.

I am a modest person. But I took off my shirt, lay on the table, heard her in the back room mixing powders and paints. She came to me carrying a small black-bellied pot inside of which was a rich red mush, slightly glittering. She adorned me. She gave me vines and flowers. She turned my body into a stake supporting whole new gardens of growth, and then, low around my hips, she painted a delicate chain-linked chastity belt. An hour later, the paint dry, I put my clothes back on, went home to film my newly wed one. This, I knew, was my gift to him, the kind of present you offer only once in your lifetime. I let him undress me.

"Wow," he said, standing back.

I blushed, and we began.

We are no longer beginning, my husband and I. This does not surprise me. Even back then, wearing the decor of desire, the serpentining tattoos, I knew they would fade, their red-clay color bleaching out until they were gone. On my wedding day I didn't care.

I do now. Eight years later, pale as a pillowcase, here I sit, with all the extra pounds and baggage time brings. And the questions have only grown more insistent. Does passion necessarily diminish over time? How reliable is romantic love, really, as a means of choosing one's mate? Can a marriage be good when Eros is replaced with friendship, or even economic partnership, two people bound by bank accounts?

Let me be clear: I still love my husband. There is no man I desire more. But it's hard to sustain romance in the crumb-filled quotidian that has become our lives. The ties that bind have been frayed by money and mortgages and children, those little imps who somehow manage to tighten the knot while weakening its actual fibers. Benjamin and I have no time for chilled white wine and salmon. The baths in our house always include Big Bird.

If this all sounds miserable, it isn't. My marriage is like a piece of comfortable clothing; even the arguments have a feel of fuzziness to them, something so familiar it can only be called home. And yet . . .

In the Western world we have for centuries concocted poems and stories and plays about the cycles of love, the way it morphs and changes over time, the way passion grabs us by our flung-back throats and then leaves us for something saner.

If *Dracula* — the frail woman, the sensuality of submission — reflects how we understand the passion of early romance, the *Flintstones* reflects our experiences of long-term love: All is gravel and somewhat silly, the song so familiar you can't stop singing it, and when you do, the emptiness is almost unbearable.

We have relied on stories to explain the complexities of love, tales of jealous gods and arrows. Now, however, these stories — so much a part of every civilization — may be changing as science steps in to explain what we have always felt to be myth, to be magic. For the first time, new research has begun to illuminate where love lies in the brain, the particulars of its chemical components.

Anthropologist Helen Fisher may be the closest we've ever come to having a doyenne of desire. At 60 she exudes a sexy confidence, with corn-colored hair, soft as floss, and a willowy build. A professor at Rutgers University, she lives in New York City, her book-lined apartment near Central Park, with its green trees fluffed out in the summer season, its paths crowded with couples holding hands.

Fisher has devoted much of her career to studying the biochemical pathways of love in all its manifestations: lust, romance, attachment, the way they wax and wane. One leg casually crossed over the other, ice clinking in her glass, she speaks with appealing frankness, discussing the ups and downs of love the way most people talk about real estate. "A woman unconsciously uses orgasms as a way of deciding whether or not a man is good for her. If he's impatient and rough, and she doesn't have the orgasm, she may instinctively feel he's less likely to be a good husband and father. Scientists think the fickle female orgasm may have evolved to help women distinguish Mr. Right from Mr. Wrong."

One of Fisher's central pursuits in the past decade has been looking at love, quite literally, with the aid of an MRI machine. Fisher and her colleagues Arthur Aron and Lucy Brown recruited subjects who had been "madly in love" for an average of seven months. Once inside the MRI machine, subjects were shown two photographs, one neutral, the other of their loved one.

What Fisher saw fascinated her. When each subject looked at his or her loved one, the parts of the brain linked to reward and pleasure — the ventral tegmental area and the caudate nucleus — lit up. What excited Fisher most was not so much finding a location, an address, for love as tracing its specific chemical pathways. Love lights up the caudate nucleus because it is home to a dense spread of receptors for a neurotransmitter called dopamine, which Fisher came to think of as part of our own endogenous love potion. In the right proportions, dopamine creates intense energy, exhilaration, focused attention, and motivation to win rewards. It is why, when you are newly in love, you can stay up all night, watch the sun rise, run a race, ski fast down a slope ordinarily too steep for your skill. Love makes you bold, makes you bright, makes you run real risks, which you sometimes survive, and sometimes you don't.

I first fell in love when I was only 12, with a teacher. His name was Mr. McArthur, and he wore open-toed sandals and sported a beard. I had never had a male teacher before, and I thought it terribly exotic. Mr. McArthur did things no other teacher dared to do. He explained to us the physics of farting. He demonstrated how to make an egg explode. He smoked cigarettes at recess, leaning languidly against the side of the school building, the ash growing longer and longer until he casually tapped it off with his finger.

What unique constellation of needs led me to love a man who made an egg explode is interesting, perhaps, but not as interesting, for me, as my memory of love's sheer physical facts. I had never felt anything like it before. I could not get Mr. McArthur out of my mind. I was anxious; I gnawed at the lining of my cheek until I tasted the tang of blood. School became at once terrifying and exhilarating. Would I see him in the hallway? In the cafeteria? I hoped. But when my wishes were granted, and I got a glimpse of my man, it satisfied nothing; it only inflamed me all the more. Had he looked at me? Why had he not looked at me? When would I see him again? At home I looked him up in the phone book; I rang him, this in a time before caller ID. He answered.

"Hello?" Pain in my heart, ripped down the middle. Hang up.

Call back. "Hello?" I never said a thing.

Once I called him at night, late, and from the way he answered the phone it was clear, even to a prepubescent like me, that he was with a woman. His voice fuzzy, the tinkle of her laughter in the background. I didn't get out of bed for a whole day.

Sound familiar? Maybe you were 30 when it happened to you, or 8 or 80 or 25. Maybe you lived in Kathmandu or Kentucky; age and geography are irrelevant. Donatella Marazziti is a professor of psychiatry at the University of Pisa in Italy who has studied the biochemistry of lovesickness. Having been in love twice herself and felt its awful power, Marazziti became interested in exploring the similarities between love and obsessive-compulsive disorder.

She and her colleagues measured serotonin levels in the blood of 24 subjects who had fallen in love within the past six months and obsessed about this love object for at least four hours every day. Serotonin is, perhaps, our star neurotransmitter, altered by our star psychiatric medications: Prozac and Zoloft and Paxil, among others. Researchers have long hypothesized that people with obsessive-compulsive disorder (OCD) have a serotonin "imbalance." Drugs like Prozac seem to alleviate OCD by increasing the amount of this neurotransmitter available at the juncture between neurons.

Marazziti compared the lovers' serotonin levels with those of a group of people suffering from OCD and another group who were free from both passion and mental illness. Levels of serotonin in both the obsessives' blood and the lovers' blood were 40 percent lower than those in her normal subjects. Translation: Love and obsessive-compulsive disorder could have a similar chemical profile. Translation: Love and mental illness may be difficult to tell apart. Translation: Don't be a fool. Stay away.

Of course that's a mandate none of us can follow. We do fall in love, sometimes over and over again, subjecting ourselves, each time, to a very sick state of mind. There is hope, however, for those caught in the grip of runaway passion — Prozac. There's nothing like that bicolored bullet for damping down the sex drive and making you feel "blah" about the buffet. Helen Fisher believes that the ingestion of drugs like Prozac jeopardizes one's ability to fall in love — and stay in love. By dulling the keen edge of love and its associated libido, relationships go stale. Says Fisher, "I know of one couple on the edge of divorce. The wife was on an antidepressant. Then she went off it, started having orgasms once more, felt the renewal of sexual attraction for her husband, and they're now in love all over again."

Psychoanalysts have concocted countless theories about why we fall in love with whom we do. Freud would have said your choice is influenced by the unrequited wish to bed your mother, if you're a boy, or your father, if you're a girl, Jung believed that passion is driven by some kind of collective unconscious. Today psychiatrists such as Thomas Lewis from the University of California at San Francisco's School of Medicine hypothesize that romantic love is rooted in our earliest infantile experiences with intimacy, how we felt at the breast, our mother's face, these things of pure unconflicted comfort that get engraved in our brain and that we ceaselessly try to recapture as adults. According to this theory we love whom we love not so much because of the future we hope to build but because of the past we hope to reclaim. Love is reactive, not proactive, it arches us backward, which may be why a certain person just "feels right." Or "feels familiar." He or she is familiar. He or she has a certain look or smell or sound or touch that activates buried memories.

> **Love and obsessive-compulsive disorder could have a similar chemical profile. Translation: Love and mental illness may be difficult to tell apart. Translation: Don't be a fool. Stay away.**

When I first met my husband, I believed this psychological theory was more or less correct. My husband has red hair and a soft voice. A chemist, he is whimsical and odd. One day before we married he dunked a rose in liquid nitrogen so it froze, whereupon he flung it against the wall, spectacularly shattering it. That's when I fell in love with him. My father, too, has red hair, a soft voice, and many eccentricities. He was prone to bursting into song, prompted by something we never saw.

However, it turns out my theories about why I came to love my husband may be just so much hogwash. Evolutionary psychology has said good riddance to Freud and the Oedipal complex and all that other transcendent stuff and hello to simple survival skills. It hypothesizes that we tend to see as attractive, and thereby choose as mates, people who look healthy. And health, say these evolutionary psychologists, is manifested in a woman with a 70 percent waistto- hip ratio and men with rugged features that suggest a strong supply of testosterone in their blood. Waist-to-hip ratio is important for the successful birth of a baby, and studies have shown this precise ratio signifies higher fertility. As for the rugged look, well, a man with a good dose of testosterone probably also has a strong immune system and so is more likely to give his partner healthy children.

Perhaps our choice of mates is a simple matter of following our noses. Claus Wedekind of the University of Lausanne in Switzerland did an interesting experiment with sweaty Tshirts. He asked 49 women to smell T-shirts previously worn by unidentified men with a variety of the genotypes that influence both body odor and immune systems. He then asked the women to rate which T-shirts smelled the best, which the worst. What Wedekind found was that women preferred the scent of a T-shirt worn by a man whose genotype was most different from hers, a genotype that, perhaps, is linked to an immune system that possesses something hers does not. In this way she increases the chance that her offspring will be robust.

It all seems too good to be true, that we are so hardwired and yet unconscious of the wiring. Because no one to my knowledge has ever said, "I married him because of his B.O." No. We say, "I married him (or her) because he's intelligent, she's beautiful, he's witty, she's compassionate." But we may just be as deluded about love as we are when we're in love. If it all comes down to a sniff test, then dogs definitely have the edge when it comes to choosing mates.

Why doesn't passionate love last? How is it possible to see a person as beautiful on Monday, and 364 days later, on another Monday, to see that beauty as bland? Surely the object of your affection could not have changed that much. She still has the same shaped eyes. Her voice has always had that husky sound, but now it grates on you — she sounds like she needs an antibiotic. Or maybe you're the one who needs an antibiotic, because the partner you once loved and cherished and saw as though saturated with starlight now feels more like a low-level infection, tiring you, sapping all your strength.

Studies around the world confirm that, indeed, passion usually ends. Its conclusion is as common as its initial flare. No wonder some cultures think selecting a lifelong mate based on something so fleeting is folly. Helen Fisher has suggested that relationships frequently break up after four years because that's about how long it takes to raise a child through infancy. Passion, that wild, prismatic insane feeling, turns out to be practical after all. We not only need to copulate; we also need enough passion to start breeding, and then feelings of attachment take over as the partners bond to raise a helpless human infant. Once a baby is no longer nursing, the child can be left with sister, aunts, friends. Each parent is now free to meet another mate and have more children.

Biologically speaking, the reasons romantic love fades may be found in the way our brains respond to the surge and pulse of dopamine that accompanies passion and makes us fly. Cocaine users describe the phenomenon of tolerance: The brain adapts to the excessive input of the drug. Perhaps the neurons become desensitized and need more and more to produce the high — to put out pixie dust, metaphorically speaking.

Maybe it's a good thing that romance fizzles. Would we have railroads, bridges, planes, faxes, vaccines, and television if we were all always besotted? In place of the ever evolving technology that has marked human culture from its earliest tool use, we would have instead only bonbons, bouquets, and birth control. More seriously, if the chemically altered state induced by romantic love is akin to a mental illness or a drug-induced euphoria, exposing yourself for too long could result in psychological damage. A good sex life can be as strong as Gorilla Glue, but who wants that stuff on your skin?

Once upon a time, in India, a boy and a girl fell in love without their parents' permission. They were from different castes, their relationship radical and unsanctioned. Picture it: the sparkling sari, the boy in white linen, the clandestine meetings on tiled terraces with a fat, white moon floating overhead. Who could deny these lovers their pleasure, or condemn the force of their attraction?

Their parents could. In one recent incident a boy and girl from different castes were hanged at the hands of their parents as hundreds of villagers watched. A couple who eloped were stripped and beaten. Yet another couple committed suicide after their parents forbade them to marry.

Anthropologists used to think that romance was a Western construct, a bourgeois by-product of the Middle Ages. Romance was for the sophisticated, took place in cafÈs, with coffees and Cabernets, or on silk sheets, or in rooms with a flickering fire. It was assumed that non- Westerners, with their broad familial and social obligations, were spread too thin for particular passions. How could a collectivist culture celebrate or in any way sanction the obsession with one individual that defines new love? Could a lice-ridden peasant really feel passion?

Easily, as it turns out. Scientists now believe that romance is panhuman, embedded in our brains since Pleistocene times. In a study of 166 cultures, anthropologists William Jankowiak and Edward Fischer observed evidence of passionate love in 147 of them. In another study men and women from Europe, Japan, and the Philippines were asked to fill out a survey to measure their experiences of passionate love. All three groups professed feeling passion with the same searing intensity.

But though romantic love may be universal, its cultural expression is not. To the Fulbe tribe of northern Cameroon, poise matters more than passion. Men who spend too much time with their wives are taunted, and those who are weak-kneed are thought to have fallen under a dangerous spell. Love may be inevitable, but for the Fulbe its manifestations are shameful, equated with sickness and social impairment.

In India romantic love has traditionally been seen as dangerous, a threat to a wellcrafted caste system in which marriages are arranged as a means of preserving lineage and bloodlines. Thus the gruesome tales, the warnings embedded in fables about what happens when one's wayward impulses take over.

Today love marriages appear to be on the rise in India, often in defiance of parents' wishes. The triumph of romantic love is celebrated in Bollywood films. Yet most Indians still believe arranged marriages are more likely to succeed than love marriages. In one survey of Indian college students, 76 percent said they'd marry someone with all the right qualities even if they weren't in love with the person (compared with only 14 percent of Americans). Marriage is considered too important a step to leave to chance.

> **Studies around the world confirm that, indeed, passion usually ends. No wonder some cultures think selecting a lifelong mate based on something so fleeting is folly.**

Renu Dinakaran is a striking 45-year-old woman who lives in Bangalore, India. When I meet her, she is dressed in Western-style clothes — black leggings and a T-shirt. Renu lives in a well-appointed apartment in this thronging city, where cows sleep on the highways as tiny cars whiz around them, plumes of black smoke rising from their sooty pipes.

Renu was born into a traditional Indian family where an arranged marriage was expected. She was not an arranged kind of person, though, emerging from her earliest days as a fierce tennis player, too sweaty for saris, and smarter than many of the men around her. Nevertheless at the age of 17 she was married off to a first cousin, a man she barely knew, a man she wanted to learn to love, but couldn't. Renu considers many arranged marriages to be acts of "state-sanctioned rape."

Renu hoped to fall in love with her husband, but the more years that passed, the less love she felt, until, at the end, she was shrunken, bitter, hiding behind the curtains of her in-laws' bungalow, looking with longing at the couple on the balcony across from theirs. "It was so obvious to me that couple had married for love, and I envied them. I really did. It hurt me so much to see how they stood together, how they went shopping for bread and eggs."

Exhausted from being forced into confinement, from being swaddled in saris that made it difficult to move, from resisting the pressure to eat off her husband's plate, Renu did what traditional Indian culture forbids one to do. She left. By this time she had had two children. She took them with her. In her mind was an old movie she'd seen on TV, a movie so strange and enticing to her, so utterly confounding and comforting at the same time, that she couldn't get it out of her head. It was 1986. The movie was *Love Story*.

"Before I saw movies like *Love Story,* I didn't realize the power that love can have," she says.

Renu was lucky in the end. In Mumbai she met a man named Anil, and it was then, for the first time, that she felt passion. "When I first met Anil, it was like nothing I'd ever experienced. He was the first man I ever had an orgasm with. I was high, just high, all the time. And I knew it wouldn't last, couldn't last, and so that infused it with a sweet sense of longing, almost as though we were watching the end approach while we were also discovering each other."

When Renu speaks of the end, she does not, to be sure, mean the end of her relationship with Anil; she means the end of a certain stage. The two are still happily married, companionable, loving if not "in love," with a playful black dachshund they bought together. Their relationship, once so full of fire, now seems to simmer along at an even temperature, enough to keep them well fed and warm. They are grateful.

"Would I want all that passion back?" Renu asks. "Sometimes, yes. But to tell you the truth, it was exhausting."

From a physiological point of view, this couple has moved from the dopamine-drenched state of romantic love to the relative quiet of an oxytocin-induced attachment. Oxytocin is a hormone that promotes a feeling of connection, bonding. It is released when we hug our long-term spouses, or our children. It is released when a mother nurses her infant. Prairie voles, animals with high levels of oxytocin, mate for life. When scientists block oxytocin receptors in these rodents, the animals don't form monogamous bonds and tend to roam. Some researchers speculate that autism, a disorder marked by a profound inability to forge and maintain social connections, is linked to an oxytocin deficiency. Scientists have been experimenting by treating autistic people with oxytocin, which in some cases has helped alleviate their symptoms.

In long-term relationships that work — like Renu and Anil's — oxytocin is believed to be abundant in both partners. In long-term relationships that never get off the ground, like Renu and her first husband's, or that crumble once the high is gone, chances are the couple has not found a way to stimulate or sustain oxytocin production.

"But there are things you can do to help it along," says Helen Fisher. "Massage. Make love. These things trigger oxytocin and thus make you feel much closer to your partner."

Well, I suppose that's good advice, but it's based on the assumption that you still want to have sex with that boring windbag of a husband. Should you fake-it-till-you-make-it?

"Yes," says Fisher. "Assuming a fairly healthy relationship, if you have enough orgasms with your partner, you may become attached to him or her. You will stimulate oxytocin."

This may be true. But it sounds unpleasant. It's exactly what your mother always said about vegetables: "Keep eating your peas. They are an acquired taste. Eventually, you will come to like them."

But I have never been a peas person.

It's 90 degrees on the day my husband and I depart, from Boston for New York City, to attend a kissing school. With two kids, two cats, two dogs, a lopsided house, and a questionable school system, we may know how to kiss, but in the rough and tumble of our harried lives we have indeed forgotten how to *kiss*.

The sky is paved with clouds, the air as sticky as jam in our hands and on our necks. The Kissing School, run by Cherie Byrd, a therapist from Seattle, is being held on the 12th floor of a rundown building in Manhattan. Inside, the room is white-washed; a tiled table holds bottles of banana and apricot nectar, a pot of green tea, breath mints, and Chapstick. The other Kissing School students — sometimes they come from as far away as Vietnam and Nigeria — are sprawled happily on the bare floor, pillows and blankets beneath them. The class will be seven hours long.

Byrd starts us off with foot rubs. "In order to be a good kisser," she says, "you need to learn how to do the foreplay before the kissing." Foreplay involves rubbing my husband's smelly feet, but that is not as bad as when he has to rub mine. Right before we left the house, I accidentally stepped on a diaper the dog had gotten into, and although I washed, I now wonder how well.

"Inhale," Byrd says, and shows us how to draw in air.

"Exhale," she says, and then she jabs my husband in the back. "Don't focus on the toes so much," she says. "Move on to the calf."

Byrd tells us other things about the art of kissing. She describes the movement of energy through various chakras, the manifestation of emotion in the lips; she describes the importance of embracing all your senses, how to make eye contact as a prelude, how to whisper just the right way. Many hours go by. My cell phone rings. It's our babysitter. Our one-yearold has a high fever. We must cut the long lesson short. We rush out. Later on, at home, I tell my friends what we learned at Kissing School: We don't have time to kiss.

A perfectly typical marriage. Love in the Western world.

Luckily I've learned of other options for restarting love. Arthur Aron, a psychologist at Stony Brook University in New York, conducted an experiment that illuminates some of the mechanisms by which people become and stay attracted. He recruited a group of men and women and put opposite sex pairs in rooms together, instructing each pair to perform a series of tasks, which included telling each other personal details about themselves. He then asked each couple to stare into each other's eyes for two minutes. After this encounter, Aron found most of the couples, previously strangers to each other, reported feelings of attraction. In fact, one couple went on to marry.

> **Novelty triggers dopamine in the brain, which can stimulate feelings of attraction. So riding a roller coaster on a first date is more likely to lead to second and third dates.**

Fisher says this exercise works wonders for some couples. Aron and Fisher also suggest doing novel things together, because novelty triggers dopamine in the brain, which can stimulate feelings of attraction. In other words, if your heart flutters in his presence, you might decide it's not because you're anxious but because you love him. Carrying this a step further, Aron and others have found that even if you just jog in place and then meet someone, you're more likely to think they're attractive. So first dates that involve a nerve-racking activity, like riding a roller coaster, are more likely to lead to second and third dates. That's a strategy worthy of posting on Match.com. Play some squash. And in times of stress — natural disasters, blackouts, predators on the prowl — lock up tight and hold your partner.

In Somerville, Massachusetts, where I live with my husband, our predators are primarily mosquitoes. That needn't stop us from trying to enter the windows of each other's soul. When I propose this to Benjamin, he raises an eyebrow.

"Why don't we just go out for Cambodian food?" he says.

"Because that's not how the experiment happened."

As a scientist, my husband is always up for an experiment. But our lives are so busy that, in order to do this, we have to make a plan. We will meet next Wednesday at lunchtime and try the experiment in our car.

On the Tuesday night before our rendezvous, I have to make an unplanned trip to New York. My husband is more than happy to forget our date. I, however, am not. That night, from my hotel room, I call him.

"We can do it on the phone," I say.

"What am I supposed to stare into?" he asks. "The keypad?"

"There's a picture of me hanging in the hall. Look at that for two minutes. I'll look at a picture I have of you in my wallet."

"Come on," he says.

"Be a sport," I say. "It's better than nothing."

Maybe not. Two minutes seems like a long time to stare at someone's picture with a receiver pressed to your ear. My husband sneezes, and I try to imagine his picture sneezing right along with him, and this makes me laugh.

Another 15 seconds pass, slowly, each second stretched to its limit so I can almost hear time, feel time, its taffy-like texture, the pop it makes when it's done. Pop pop pop. I stare and stare at my husband's picture. It doesn't produce any sense of startling intimacy, and I feel defeated.

Still, I keep on. I can hear him breathing on the other end. The photograph before me was taken a year or so ago, cut to fit my wallet, his strawberry blond hair pulled back in a ponytail. I have never really studied it before. And I realize that in this picture my husband is not looking straight back at me, but his pale blue eyes are cast sideways, off to the left, looking at something I can't see. I touch his eyes. I peer close, and then still closer, at his averted face. Is there something sad in his expression, something sad in the way he gazes off?

I look toward the side of the photo, to find what it is he's looking at, and then I see it: a tiny turtle coming toward him. Now I remember how he caught it after the camera snapped, how he held it gently in his hands, showed it to our kids, stroked its shell, his forefinger moving over the scaly dome, how he held the animal out toward me, a love offering. I took it, and together we sent it back to the sea.

14

DYSFUNCTIONAL COMMUNICATION
AND WHAT TO DO ABOUT IT

ROWLAND S. MILLER • DANIEL PERLMAN • SHARON S. BREHM

As we've seen, the more open and self-disclosing spouses are to one another, the more happily married they tend to be (Meeks et al., 1998). But not all our efforts to speak our minds and communicate with our partners have positive results. More often than we realize, we face an interpersonal gap that causes misunderstanding or confusion in those who hear what we have to say. And the nature and consequences of miscommunication are very apparent in relationships in which the partners are distressed and dissatisfied. The verbal communications of unhappy partners often just perpetuate their discontent and make things worse instead of better.

Miscommunication

Indeed, we can gain valuable insights about what we shouldn't do when we talk with others by carefully comparing the communicative behaviors of happy lovers to those of unhappy partners. John Gottman and his colleagues at the University of Washington have been doing this for over 30 years, and they have observed several important patterns. First, unhappy people do a poor job of *saying what they mean* (Gottman, 1994b). When they have a complaint, they are rarely precise; instead, they're prone to **kitchen-sinking,** in which they tend to address several topics at once (so that everything but the "kitchen sink" gets dragged into the conversation). This usually causes their primary concern to get lost in the barrage of frustrations that are announced at the same time. If they're annoyed by late fees at the video store, for instance, they may say, "It's not just your carelessness, it's those friends you hang out with, and your lousy attitude about helping out around the house." As a result, their conversations frequently drift **off-beam,** wandering from topic to topic so that the conversation never stays on one problem long enough to resolve it: "You never do what I ask. You're just as hard-headed as your mother, and you always take her side." Flitting from problem to problem on a long list of concerns makes it almost certain that none of them will be fixed.

Second, unhappy partners do a poor job of *hearing each other*. They rarely try to patiently double-check their understanding of their partners' messages. Instead, they jump to conclusions (often assuming the worst) and head off on tangents based on what they presume their partners really mean. One aspect of this is **mindreading,** which occurs when people assume that they understand their partners' thoughts, feelings, and opinions without asking. All intimate couples mindread to some extent, but distressed couples do so in critical and hostile ways; they tend to perceive unpleasant motives where neutral or positive ones actually exist: "You just said that to make me mad, to get back at me for yesterday." Unhappy partners also **interrupt** each other in negative ways more than contented couples do. Not all interruptions are obnoxious. People who interrupt their partners to express agreement or ask for clarification may actually be communicating happily and well. But people who interrupt to express disagreement or to change the topic are likely to leave their partners feeling disregarded and unappreciated (Daigen & Holmes, 2000).

Distressed couples also listen poorly by finding something wrong or unworkable with anything their partners say. This is **yes-butting,** and it communicates constant criticism of the others' points of view: "Yeah, we could try that, but it won't work because . . ." Unhappy partners also engage in **cross-complaining** that fails to acknowledge others' concerns; instead of expressing interest in what their partners have to say, they just respond to a complaint with one of their own:

"I hate the way you let the dishes pile up in the sink."

"Well, I hate the way you leave your clothes lying around on the floor."

Finally, unhappy partners too often display *negative affect* when they talk with each other (Gottman & Levenson, 1992). They often react to their partner's complaints with sarcastic disregard that is demeaning and scornful, and instead of mending their problems, they often make them worse. Damaging interactions like these typically begin with **criticism** that attacks a partner's personality or character instead of identifying a specific behavior that is causing concern. For instance, instead of delineating a particular frustration ("I get annoyed when you leave your wet towels on the floor"), a critic may inflame the interaction by making a global accusation of a character flaw ("You are such a slob!"). **Contempt** in the form of insults, mockery, or hostile humor is often involved as well. The partners' common response to such attacks is **defensiveness;** instead of treating the clumsy complaint as legitimate and reasonable, the partners seek to protect themselves from the perceived attack by making excuses or by cross-complaining, hurling counterattacks of their own. **Stonewalling** may follow, particularly in men, as a partner "clams up" and reacts to the messy situation by withdrawing into a stony silence (Heavy, Layne, & Christensen, 1993). People may believe they're helping the situation by refusing to argue further, but their lack of responsiveness can be infuriating (Zadro & Williams, 2000). Instead of demonstrating appropriate acknowledgement and concern for a partner's complaints, stonewalling typically communicates "disapproval, icy distance, and smugness" (Gottman, 1994b, p. 94). Ultimately, destructive **belligerence** may occur, with one partner aggressively rejecting the other altogether ("So what? What are you gonna do about it?").

When communication routinely degenerates into these contentious patterns, the outlook for the relationship is grim (Gottman et al., 1998). In fact, videotapes of just the first three minutes of a marital conflict enable researchers to predict with 83 percent accuracy who will be divorced six years later (Carrère & Gottman, 1999). Couples whose marriages are doomed display noticeably more contempt, defensiveness, and belligerence than do those who will stay together. And among those who stay together, spouses who communicate well are happier and more content than those who suffer frequent misunderstanding (Feeney, 1994).

The challenge, of course, is that it's not always easy to avoid these problems. When we're angry, resentful, or anxious, we may find ourselves cross-complaining, kitchen-sinking, and all the rest. How can we avoid these traps? Depending on the situation, we may need to send clearer, less inflammatory messages, listen better, or stay polite and calm, and sometimes we need to do all three.

Saying What We Mean

Complaints that criticize a partner's personality or character disparage the partner and often make mountains out of molehills, portraying problems as huge, intractable dilemmas that cannot be easily solved. (Given some of the broad complaints we throw at our partners, it's no wonder that they sometimes get defensive.) It's much more sensible — and accurate — to identify as plainly and concretely as possible a specific behavior that annoyed us. This is **behavior description,** and it not only tells our partners what's on our minds, it focuses the conversation on discrete, manageable behaviors that, unlike personalities, can often be readily changed. A good behavior description specifies a particular event and does not involve generalities; thus, words such as *always* or *never* should never be used. This is *not* a good behavior description: "You're always interrupting me! You never let me finish!"

We should also use **I-statements** that specify our feelings. I-statements start with "I" and then describe a distinct emotional reaction. They force us to identify our feelings, which can be useful both to us and our partners. They also help us to "own" our feelings and acknowledge them instead of keeping the entire focus on the partner. Thus, instead of saying, "You really piss me off," one should say, "I feel pretty angry right now."

A handy way to use both behavior descriptions and I-statements to communicate more clearly and accurately is to integrate them into **XYZ statements.** Such statements follow the form of "When you do **X** in situation **Y**" (that's a good behavior description), "I feel **Z**" (an I-statement). Listen to yourself next time you complain to your partner. Are you saying something like this:

"You're so inconsiderate! You never let me finish what I'm saying!"

Or, are you being precise and accurate and saying what you mean:

"When you interrupted me just now, I felt annoyed."

There's a big difference. One of those statements is likely to get a thoughtful, apologetic response from a loving partner, but the other probably won't.

Active Listening

We have two vital tasks when we're on the receiving end of others' messages. The first is to accurately understand what our partners are trying to say, and the second is to communicate that attention and comprehension to our partners so that they know we care about what they've said. Both tasks can be accomplished by **paraphrasing** a message, repeating it in our own words and giving the sender a chance to agree that that's what he or she actually meant. When people use paraphrasing, they don't assume that they understood their partners and issue an immediate reply. Instead, they take a moment to check their comprehension by rephrasing the message and repeating it back. This sounds awkward, but it is a terrific way to avoid arguments and conflict that would otherwise result from misunderstanding and mistakes. Whenever a conversation begins to get heated, paraphrasing can keep it from getting out of hand. Look what's wrong here:

WILMA: (sighing) I'm so glad your mother decided not to come visit us next week.

FRED: (irate) What's wrong with my mother? You've always been on her case, and I think you're an ungrateful witch!

Perhaps before Fred flew off the handle, some paraphrasing would have been helpful:

WILMA: (sighing) I'm so glad your mother decided not to come visit us next week.

FRED: (irate) Are you saying you don't like her to be here?

WILMA: (surprised) No, she's always welcome. I just have my paper due in my relationships class and won't have much time then.

FRED: (mollified) Oh.

Another valuable listening skill is **perception checking,** which is the opposite of mindreading. In perception checking, people assess the accuracy of their inferences about a partner's feelings by asking the partner for clarification. This communicates one's attentiveness and interest, and it encourages the partner to be more open: "You seem pretty upset by what I said, is that right?"

Listeners who paraphrase and check their perceptions make an *active* effort to understand their partners, and that care and consideration is usually much appreciated. Active listening is also likely to help smooth the inevitable rough spots any relationship encounters. Indeed, people who practice these techniques typically report happier marriages than do those who simply assume that they understand what their partners mean by what they say (Markman, Stanley, & Blumberg, 1994).

REFERENCES

Carrè re, S. & Gottman, J. M. (1999). Predicting divorce among newlyweds from the first three minutes of a marital conflict discussion. *Family Process, 38,* 293-301.

Daigen, V. & Holmes, J. G. (2000). Don't interrupt! A good rule for marriage? *Personal Relationships, 7,* 185-201.

Feeney, J. A. (1994). Attachment style, communication patterns and satisfaction across the life cycle of marriage. *Personal Relationships, 1,* 333-348.

Gottman, J. M. (1994b). *Why marriages succeed or fail.* New York: Simon & Schuster.

Gottman, J. M. & Levenson, R. W. (1992). Marital processes predictive of later dissolution: Behavior, physiology and health. *Journal of Personality and Social Psychology, 63,* 221-233.

Gottman, J. M., Coan, J., Carrè re, S. & Swanson, C. (1998). Predicting marital happiness and stability from newlywed interactions. *Journal of Marriage and the Family, 60,* 5-22.

Heavy, C. L., Layne, C. & Christensen, A. (1993). Gender and conflict structure in marital interaction: A replication and extension. *Journal of Consulting and Clinical Psychology, 61,* 16-27.

Markman, H., Stanley, S. & Blumberg, S. L. (1994). *Fighting for your marriage: Positive steps for preventing divorce and preserving a lasting love.* San Francisco: Jossey-Bass.

Meeks, B. S., Hendrick, S. S. & Hendrick, C. (1998). Communication, love and relationship satisfaction. *Journal of Personal and Social Relationships, 15,* 755-773.

Rowland S. Miller, *Intimate Relationships,* 7th Edition. Pp 166-171. Copyright (c) 2015 by McGraw-Hill Education. Used with permission of McGraw-Hill Education.

Zadro, L. & Williams, K. D. (June 2000). *The silent treatment: Ostracism in intimate relationships.* Paper presented at the meeting of the International Society for The Study of Personal Relationships, Brisbane.

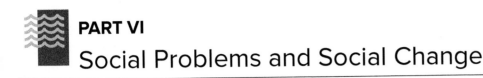

PART VI

Social Problems and Social Change

15

RELATED CONCEPTS AND IDEAS

LISA GREY WHITAKER

Personal Problems vs. Social Problems

Asocial problem is different than a personal problem. In distinguishing between the two, C. Wright Mills (1959/2000) noted that personal problems have to do with the individual and his/her immediate milieu; whereas *social problems* affect people society-wide.

Social Change

Social change is change that affects an entire social system – an entire nation (e.g. legalization of marijuana across the U.S.), global region (e.g. the impact of ISIS in the Middle East), or perhaps the entire world (e.g. the invention of the internet). Social change begins when a subset of social system's members interact and decide that a significant problem exists, about which something has to be done.

You will note that the word *change* is a neutral term. It does not necessarily connote an improvement in conditions, or at least, not an improvement from the point of view of everyone who is affected by it. Whether or not a certain type of change constitutes an improvement in conditions is relative. Like beauty, it is in the eye of the beholder. For example, from the point of view of ISIS leaders, the regions they are operating in have changed for the better since they stepped up their activities therein. For the families of the individuals ISIS has abducted, beheaded, burned alive or otherwise killed – not so much.

Social change does not necessarily have a desirable outcome from *any* group's perspective. Sometimes two interest groups, who hold mutually-exclusive ideas of what would constitute an improvement in social conditions, vie for dominance in a region and neither side ever wins. Neither side is ever able to definitively effect the changes it desires; the conflict just goes on and on. In the region where it is located, the Israeli-Palestinian conflict exemplifies this situation.

Functionalist Perspective on Social Change

Functionalists believe social change occurs when change becomes necessary for the survival of the overall social system. Inevitably, structural strains develop in the system that must be alleviated. Strains could be caused by such things as:

- Changes in the environment/ecosystem brought on by global warming, natural disasters, nuclear accidents, destruction of natural resources, etc.
- Introduction of new values, beliefs, technologies or other types of innovations/inventions into the system from outside of it, which conflict with conventional wisdom and/or traditional ways of doing things
- Inconsistencies between general societal values/governmental policies and the actual behavior of some societal members (e.g. the lip service paid to the value of equal opportunity/Title IX mandates vis à vis the discrimination against women and minorities practiced by some societal members).

- Conflicting beliefs, values, priorities, etc. held by various interest groups *within* the social system, which prompt each group to hold distinct and conflicting views on how things should be done in the social system.

From the functionalist point of view, the changes that take place in response to such strains are the types of adjustments and adaptations required to alleviate systemic stresses.

Conflict Perspective on Social Change

Conflict theorists focus on processes of change that are efforts to resolve the inequality between various member groups in the system. Along with wealth and material possessions, social class, social status, social power and influence, political power and influence, media power and influence, etc. are also viewed as scarce resources. Each interest group strives to get a bigger share of the existing resources than it already has while holding onto whatever resources they do have.

Conflict theorists note that the Elites of society, who control the majority of the resources, use cultural values, beliefs, frames of reference and the media as tools — some would say weapons — to keep what they have. As an example, the Tea Party very successfully used "The American Dream" frame of reference and the "No New Taxes!" slogan to get a lot of poor people to vote against their own interests. Those voters did not understand that by "No New Taxes!" the rich were talking about not being taxed *themselves*. By keeping taxes low for the rich and eliminating or reducing many taxes that were previously in place, monies that might have been applied to social programs evaporated or never became available.

Conflict theorists believe the pastimes offered by popular culture — reality TV, game shows, soap operas, schlock movies, Facebook, Twitter, surfing the internet, chat rooms, playing the lottery, casino and other forms of gambling, video gaming, participation in virtual-reality worlds, 24-7 online shopping, etc. — well-serve the interests of Society's Elites. Popular culture diverts the attention of the masses from the realities of inequality; for example, that most people do *not* have a say in how society is run. More specifically, the masses do not have access to the higher-level conversations wherein decisions are made about what issues and whose viewpoints get media and legislative attention, about how opportunities to participate in public life are distributed, about how many other types of opportunities (for housing, schooling, jobs, etc.) and other forms of resources are distributed. In the conflict view, once diverted by popular culture, the common folk are less likely to question or challenge the status quo, less likely to rise up and cause trouble in the form of social and political activism.

Interactionist Perspective on Social Change

Interactionists believe that to understand social change, you must begin by examining the meaning that each of the different groups involved in the change give to the context in which the change efforts take place, and to the outcome of those efforts itself. Those groups include:

- Persons who work to bring about the change
- Persons who work to prevent the change from happening
- Persons who are impacted by the change efforts and end result
- Bystanders who look on while change efforts are in-progress but do not care about or have any stake in the way things turn out

Interactionists believe that in order to effect a type of social change, the activist group must:

- Form a collective identity — Members must come to see themselves as a unit of persons who share specific interests and goals.
- Agree upon and define a specific problem in need of remedy
- Create or adopt some buzzwords or a phrase as the group's slogan which, on the surface, any fool would think was a good thing. Then, utter this slogan a lot. An example of this would be the NRA advocating Preserve our Constitutional rights!' in their efforts to prevent stronger gun control in the U.S.
- Come up with a concrete plan — Members must agree upon and lay out a specific course of action or actions to bring about the type of change that, as they see it, will solve the problem.

- Successfully recruit an adequate number of new members to the group, including those with particular skills or access the group needs
- Get persons in power in local government, business, the media, etc. to legitimate, endorse and facilitate attainment of the group's goal(s)

Collective Behavior and Social Change

Collective behavior is relatively short-lived action taken by an aggregate of persons who in all likelihood do not know each other, but who are brought together in the same physical space due to a common interest in some activity that is in progress there. Those individuals then decide to 'do something' in order to (a) solve a problem they perceive has arisen or (b) fulfill a need/achieve a goal they temporarily share. The group disbands once have accomplished their purpose.

All of us engage in many forms of collective behavior over our lifetimes. Crowd behavior, such as is fueled by the emotional momentum that builds among fans at a football game; gossip and rumor-spreading, dressing or wearing your hair in accordance with the latest fad or fashion; even crowd behavior in panic situations, are all forms of collective behavior.

While members of most collectives never get to know each other or form lasting social bonds, there are exceptions. Under extreme conditions, such as wartime combat or havoc wrought by a natural or manmade disaster, strangers will pull together to survive until help arrives. During an ordeal wherein emotions run high and deep; surviving by their cooperative actions, strangers may well become bonded for life.

Collective behavior may ensue to fill a gap in information that is making everyone concerned anxious. For example, among employees of a company that, according to the morning newspaper, is in serious financial trouble, collective action may take the form of rumors and gossip around the break room. Once the immediate need is taken care of – the company owner meets with and assures her employees that both the company and their jobs are on solid ground – the employees disband and go about their business.

Collective behavior can lead to social change without enduring to the point of becoming a social movement. The Watts Riots of 1965, in Los Angeles, are a case in point. However destructive those riots and subsequent looting activity were in the immediate sense, for the people who lived there, as a historical event they were catalysts for social reforms that benefited the people of Watts, as well as minorities and the socio-economically deprived generally. In the wake of such a manifestation of rage and frustration, even more complacent if not comatose members of the legislature and public were awakened to the reality that *something had to be done.*

Social Movements and Social Change

Social change may occur through the activities of a *social movement*. Unlike more ephemeral groups such as those that engage in collective behavior, social movements endure over time in order to address recurrent needs, such as the havoc wrought by a geographic region's annual hurricane or tornado 'season,' or to address an ongoing social problem, such as global warming or social inequality.

A movement initially forms when people identify a problem and decide it is of sufficient magnitude and importance that they need to organize and take action to resolve it. Through ongoing interaction, members define the problem as they see it, then discuss and agree upon a course of action to remedy the problem.

By acting cooperatively over time, movement members will develop a social organization, division of labor, status hierarchy, chain of command and strategies to produce or acquire resources necessary for the group's continued operation. They develop a set of goals, norms, values, beliefs, special vocabulary and perhaps, some sort of uniform and/or a publicly-articulated mission that identifies them as a unique social unit.

A movement's membership must work out a strategy for selling their conception of the problem and proposed remedy to others, in order to accomplish their change goals. Movements need to expand their membership base in order to do the various types of work that are vital to the organization's cause. Too, in order to get those with political power to make any necessary changes in the law or public policy, so that the path to change is cleared, the movement's members will try to persuade a *majority* of society's members that their position is valid. Once a majority of citizens get behind the movement's cause, movement members can press their legislators to "do something" about the problem.

Social movements may or may not succeed in bringing about the changes they seek. As noted by the conflict theorists, gaining popular support per se is not guaranteed and even if gained, it may not be sufficient to get legislative attention and support for the changes the movement is advocating. Many behind-the-scenes factors are in play. The reality is that who does and does not get to participate in high-level decision-making matters. It matters a lot.

REFERENCES

Collins, Randall, *Conflict Sociology: Toward an Explanatory Science;* New York: Academic Press, 1975.

Conot, Robert; *Rivers of Blood, Years of Darkness;* New York: Morrow, 1968.

Harper, Charles L. and Kevin T. Leicht, *Exploring Social Change: America and The World,* fifth edition; Upper Saddle River, NJ: Pearson Prentice Hall, 2007.

Marx, Gary T. and Douglas McAdam, *Collective Behavior and Social Movements: Process and Structure;* Englewood Cliffs, NJ: Prentice Hall, 1994.

Mills, C. Wright; "The Promise," from *Sociological Imagination;* New York: Oxford University Press, 1959/2000.

Parsons, Talcott, *The Social System,* Glencoe, IL: Free Press, 1951.

_____, Societies: *Evolutionary and Comparative Perspectives,* Englewood Cliffs, NJ: Prentice Hall, 1966.

Turner, Ralph H. and Lewis M. Killian, *Collective Behavior,* Englewood Cliffs, NJ: Prentice-Hall, Second Edition, 1972.

Meinzahn/Getty Images

16

A NEW END, A NEW BEGINNING

Prepare for Life as We Don't Know It

JOHN L. PETERSEN

Learning Outcomes

After reading this article, you will be able to:

- Understand the problems and systems failures that will require a major transformation to very different systems.
- Evaluate the capacity of our government to deal with today's problems.
- Explain why governments fail.

Predicting the future is a fool's errand. It is fraught with so much complexity and uncertainty that the best one can do with integrity is to array potential alternatives – scenarios – across the horizon, and then try to think about what might be done if one of those alternative worlds materializes.

"The End Is Near" has always been doomsayers' favorite slogan, but is it now finally true? The trends suggest the end of an era may indeed be near, as growing complexity and proliferating crises threaten to obliterate "life as we know it." The time is now to prepare for the life we don't yet know.

Scenario planning has certainly been an effective discipline, helping many organizations to imagine potentialities that probably otherwise wouldn't have shown up in their field of view. But as I facilitate organizations going through these exercises, the little, nagging voice in the back of my head is not asking, "What is the array of possible futures?" Rather, it is always wondering, "What is the future really going to be?" We want concreteness. We want predictions.

I think that no one knows for sure what the future will bring, but after some time of being in the "future business," one begins to be able to discriminate between what is substantive and structural and what is largely speculative. For me, at least, some things have an intuitive sense of being real and important, and the rest of the possibilities lack just enough gravitas that I know they're only "ideas." That intuitive sense is supported when it becomes possible to triangulate from a number of independent sources that all point to the same conclusion.

People always ask me after my talks, "With all of these converging trends, what is 2012 really going to look like?" It happened again in a recent radio interview. Mostly I hedge and dance a bit and say that I don't know for sure, but I believe there will be a new world, and a new human will come out of all of the current turmoil. The notion of cooperation will shape the way people see themselves and the rest of the world, and there will be new institutions and functions, etc. Pretty general stuff.

But, over a year ago, the notion that all of this big change could spell a substantial reconfiguration of the familiar country that I have lived in all of my life began to gel in a way that moved that notion beyond being just a possibility – a wild card – into the realm of plausibility. I now have come to believe that such a transformation is likely and will happen – soon.

Ideas like this are so big and disruptive that it is really quite hard to get to the place where we take them seriously. For most of us, our lives are evolutionary – punctuated, perhaps with trauma now and then, but mostly populated by events that are familiar, even if they don't always make personal sense. The concept that everything might change is so foreign to any experience that most of us have ever had that, even if we say the words and talk about the possibility, we really don't internalize what this might mean.

Certain other thinkers jumped to the natural conclusion quite some time ago. Dmitry Orlov, for example, first started to build a theory of superpower collapse that included the United States in 1995. Only in the last few years has he been talking publicly about his ideas and the ultimate direction of U.S. trends.

James Howard Kunstler, a wonderfully entertaining and provocative writer, was very clear about the systemic and structural nature of the larger problem in his 2006 book, *The Long Emergency*. He clearly sees the demise of America coming this way. His always interesting blog is a weekly assessment of where we're going wrong.

My colleague David Martin outlined the financial dominoes that were going to fall in a talk at The Arlington Institute in July 2006. Implicit in his treatise is the collapse of the U.S. and global financial systems, but again, it's one thing to hear such views and quite another to really believe them.

After I listened to such people and pondered what they said, I began telling my friends that I thought we were seeing the beginning of the end of the United States as we've known it. I didn't think they really believed it, at least initially, but recently we have seen Singapore, for instance, reportedly making major leadership changes in its government investment company to reposition the nation away from the United States and the U.S. dollar.

Huge, extraordinary, global trends . . . are converging to precipitate a historic big transition event.

Indicators of Big Change Ahead

There are numerous indicators that suggest the big change is coming:

- **Multiple trends are converging.** Huge, extraordinary, global trends, any number of which would be enough to derail our present way of life, are converging to precipitate a historic big transition event. A partial list would include:

  - The global financial system is collapsing. During the next few months, it appears that wave after wave of blows will strike the system, raising the very real possibility that it will experience large-scale failure sometime before the end of the year.
  - We have reached the beginning of the end of petroleum. Global production has been flat for the last three years. Senior oil company executives are now saying that they will not be able to pump more. Supply will likely begin to decrease significantly after we move across the peak. Prices will increase again if the demand holds up. This is important because our present way of life is built upon petroleum.
  - The global climate system is changing — some say it is getting much warmer, others now suggest a mini ice age within the next decade. In any case, increased irregularities in local climates will probably result, with attendant problems in agriculture, natural disasters, and economies.
  - The cost of food is increasing rapidly as a result of global shortages not seen in 40 or 50 years. This could be exacerbated by increasing energy costs and climate changes. Lester R. Brown of the Earth Policy Institute believes that food shortages may bring down civilizations.
  - The effects of larger solar eruptions hitting the earth through tears in the magnetosphere surrounding our planet will likely disrupt global communications, weather, perhaps satellites, and even organic life over the next three to four years.

- **Problems are much larger than government.** Peak oil, climate change, and the financial meltdown all have the potential to significantly overwhelm the capabilities of government to respond to them. If bureaucracies can't deal with the aftermath of a natural disaster like Katrina, something ten or more times that damaging would leave most people fending for themselves. If these extraordinary, disruptive events end up being concurrent, then the whole system will be at risk.

- **The problems are structural.** They're systemic. Some of these issues, especially the financial, oil, and food problems, are also a product of how we live, our priorities, and our paradigms. We are creating the problems because of our values and principles. Without extraordinary, fundamental changes in the way we see ourselves and the world, we will keep getting what we are getting.

- **Leaders think the old system can be "rebooted."** Almost everyone in leadership positions in the Obama administration and in other countries wants to make the old system well again. Jim Kunstler has said it well:

Among the questions that disturb the sleep of many casual observers is how come Mr. O doesn't get that the conventional process of economic growth — based, as it was, on industrial expansion via revolving credit in a cheap-energy-resource era — is over, and why does he keep invoking it at the podium? Dear Mr. President, you are presiding over an epochal contraction, not a pause in the growth epic. Your assignment is to manage that contraction in a way that does not lead to world war, civil disorder or both. Among other things, contraction means that all the activities of everyday life need to be downscaled including standards of living, ranges of commerce, and levels of governance.

"Consumerism" is dead. Revolving credit is dead — at least at the scale that became normal the last thirty years. The wealth of several future generations has already been spent and there is no equity left there to refinance.

The above indicators of change suggest the reasons behind the following.

- **We're not dealing with the structural issues.** All of the biggest efforts are attempts to reinflate the financial bubble and to keep the mortally wounded institutions alive. The knee-jerk reactions come from the same people who helped to design and feed the present system. These people are also deluded — they think (or act like) they know what they are doing. They don't realize that . . .
- **The situation is so complex that no one really understands it.** The Global Business Network's Peter Schwartz, reporting on a conversation with the *Financial Times 's* Martin Wolf, said that Wolf's key point was that the nature and scale of the credit crisis is so novel that it's not clear we know what we're doing when we try to stop it. He is deeply worried. Steve Roach of Morgan Stanley said at the World Economic Forum annual meeting at Davos that he agreed with Wolf: We are in uncharted waters. Nassim Nicholas Taleb, author of *The Black Swan: Impact of the Highly Improbable* (Random House, 2007), says the financial system is so complex that it is impossible for anyone to understand it, and because of that complexity it is inevitable that it will exhibit significant, unanticipated behaviors (his Black Swans) that career across the planet.
- **The issues are global.** Economies are contracting around the world, with a huge rise in unemployment. Japan's exports are falling, and factories are closing in China, which means that products aren't being shipped.
- **The system is fundamentally out of balance.** Common sense is largely absent from many big, sweeping U.S. government edicts. The Transportation Security Administration, for example, wants to make pilots produce background checks on members of their family (and their business associates) in order to legally give them rides in noncommercial, private airplanes. The Agriculture Department wants all small farmers to put GPS/RFID tags on all of their animals so that chickens, cows, horses, and goats can be tracked, on a day-today basis, by the government. And most of the U.S. federal budget goes to the military and military-related agencies. This kind of growth, of course, is what brought down the Soviet Union.

Why Government Fails to Respond to Challenge

If the natural solutions to these massive issues include innovation, foresight, adaptability, sustainability, and resilience, it is unlikely that a thinking American could be found who would suggest that the source for these capabilities would be our government. Those who are in charge have no new ideas about how this all should work. They're also slow, and this situation needs fast, agile responses. There is an additional problem. Even if it did have good ideas, the government wouldn't be able to effectively implement them because:

- **It suffers from too much inertia, and too many lawyers and lobbyists.** There is a huge, well-funded effort in place to maintain the status quo or to shift the future to benefit one group at the expense of others. It would be impossible within the present system to initiate dramatic change when the threat was still on the horizon. Every group or organization that might be negatively affected would fight in Congress and the courts to keep themselves alive, regardless of what was at stake for the larger community. Only when the crisis was about to crash down on everyone — when adequate time and resources for effective response were nonexistent — might everyone pull together for the common good.
- **Potential solutions take too long to implement.** These issues are so gigantic that confronting and redirecting them takes a long time. One study, for example, suggested that a national crash program to find alternatives for oil would need to have been started 20 years before the peak, in order that there will be no significant disruption of the underlying systems. We do not operate with either that foresight or that resolve.
- **Supply chains are long and thin.** Globalism and just-in-time production have produced supply chains in most areas of commerce that are very long — often to the other side of the earth — and very fragile. There are many places between there and here where something can go wrong. If and when that happens, necessities will not be available. In those situations, people resort to unconventional and/or antisocial behavior.
- **Six hundred trillion dollars in derivatives is a house of cards.** Looming over the whole financial situation is an almost unfathomable quantity of financial instruments — derivatives — which are essentially casino bets with no underlying

value supporting the transaction. Warren Buffett calls them "financial weapons of mass destruction," and they could bring the whole system down. Derivatives only work if there is confidence in the system – you believe the casino will really pay your winnings. If other things in the environment erode that confidence, there is the real possibility that things will rapidly fall to pieces.

- **Cooperation is unlikely; protectionism will prevail.** Instead of countries cooperating with each other to deal with these big transnational problems, we're seeing a pulling back to protect each country's perceived shortterm interests, regardless of what the implications might be in the longer term. At the same time, we're all connected to each other in very complicated ways, so if any substantial pieces of the system don't work, it will affect all of the other ones.
- **History says it's time.** Perhaps what is most compelling to me is that history strongly suggests that the time is right for an upset – they always happen about now in the historical cycles. Big punctuations in the equilibrium of evolution have produced extraordinary, fundamental reorganizations to life on this planet on a regular, accelerating basis from the beginning of time as we know it. We make progress as a species when we are forced in one way or another to evolve into seeing ourselves and the world in new ways. Necessity is the mother of invention – or should be!

So, it doesn't look to me like we're going to be able to do what might be needed to maintain the present system. It is likely that we're at one of those extraordinary moments in history when each of us gets the opportunity to play an important role in not only transitioning to a new world, but also designing it.

What to Do in the Face of Unprecedented Change

Two specific actions come to mind that should help individuals and institutions prepare for this change.

1. **Plan for the transition.** Start to think now about how you're going to provide for yourself and those who are important to you in a time when many things don't work the way they always have in the past. There are many websites and books on this subject, but the key concept is cooperation. You can't do this alone. Start to work together with like-minded individuals to sustain yourself, regardless of whether your concerns are food, water, shelter, transportation, or finances.
2. **Start thinking about the new world.** Now is the time to begin contemplating the design of the new world. Governments should be doing this. Companies should start skunk works. Big international organizations should put it on their agendas.

Here's the catch. This might not happen. The "system" might not collapse. Personally, I think that if there is any one person that has the potential to at least soften this transition it is Barack Obama. As I've suggested, he will have his hands full just trying to get the underlying people and institutions to think differently and act fast enough, but if anyone has the chance to pull it off, he would be the one. Already, he's getting the government to move faster and in more substantive ways than any of his predecessors. It may be, by the way, that he will be the best person to wind down the old system and develop a new one. It's all of the other folks running the government that I'd be concerned about – the ones who continue to see the world as it used to be.

There are any number of reasons why this scenario might not manifest itself, not least of which is that there will be many thousands, if not millions, of people who will be working very hard to assure that the system doesn't come apart (but then, they may be doing the wrong things).

It seems to me, therefore, that flexibility and permeability (allowing new ideas to get through) are of critical importance here. Remember the first law of Discordianism: "Convictions cause convicts." Whatever you believe imprisons you.

So, stay loose. The winners need to transcend, not try to work their way through all of this. Concentrate on building the new world. Don't get emotionally involved in the daily reports of the current global erosion.

ADDITIONAL RESOURCES

America's Defense Meltdown: Pentagon Reform for President Obama and the New Congress, edited by Winslow Wheeler (Stanford Security Studies, 2009). In sharp contrast to the political apparatchiks protesting that more money is needed to reverse the shrinking, aging, and declining readiness of the Army, Navy, and Air Force, few seem to understand that budget increases are a primary cause of the problems, a symptom clearly described in this new book.

"Asymmetric Collateral Damage: Basel II, the Mortgage House of Cards, and the Coming Economic Crisis," a talk by David Martin, CEO of M.CAM, for The Arlington Institute (July 12, 2006), www.arlingtoninstitute.org/dr-david-e-martin.

Crash Course, a "concise video seminar on how our economy, energy systems, and environment interact, and how they will impact the future," at www.chrismartenson.com.

Reinventing Collapse by Dmitry Orlov (New Society, 2008).

A Vision for 2012: *Planning for Extraordinary Change* by John L. Petersen (Fulcrum Publishing, 2008).

"Why Obama's 'Rescue' Misses the Mark and the Coming Financial Collapse Just Got Worse" by David Martin of M.CAM (February 15, 2009), http://invertedalchemy.blogspot.com/.

CRITICAL THINKING

1. Do you agree with Petersen's thesis that "Problems are larger than government"?
2. What course of action would you propose in the situation that Petersen describes?
3. Can you refute the thesis of the demise of America?

CREATE CENTRAL

www.mhhe.com/createcentral

INTERNET REFERENCES

Sociosite
www.topsite.com/goto/sociosite.net

Socioweb
www.topsite.com/goto/socioweb.com

Sociology – Study Sociology Online
http://edu.learnsoc.org

Sociology Web Resources
www.mhhe.com/socscience/sociology/resources/index.htm

John L. Petersen is president of The Arlington Institute, a nonprofit, future-oriented think tank. Among his books are WFS bestsellers *The Road to 2015* (1994), *Out of the Blue* (1997), and *A Vision for 2012* (2008). His address is The Arlington Institute, P.O. Box 86, Berkeley Springs, West Virginia 25411. E-mail johnp@arlingtoninstitute.org. Petersen also discussed these ideas in a chapter of the World Future Society's 2009 conference volume, *Innovation and Creativity in a Complex World,* which may be ordered from www.wfs.org/wfsbooks.htm.

Notes

Notes

Notes

Notes

Notes